100 Things I Meant to Tell You

100 THINGS
I Meant to Tell You

Arthur Smith

Published by AA Media Limited, whose registered office is
Grove House, Lutyens Close, Basingstoke, Hampshire RG24 8AG;
registered number 06112600

First published in 2019

A CIP catalogue record for this book is available from the British Library.

ISBN: 978-0-7495-8194-7

Publisher: Phil Carroll
Editor: Donna Wood
Art Director: James Tims
Designer: Tracey Freestone

Printed and bound in the UK by Clays Ltd

A05704

theAA.com

For Beth

Now and forever

Contents

Introduction   13

1 - Grumpy Old Man   17

2 - How to Cope with Hecklers   21

3 - Walking into Gainsborough   25

4 - Ken and Doug   29

5 - Eighty   32

6 - If (by Arthur Kipling)   35

7 - Passenger Announcement   36

8 - The Joy of Not Going   39

9 - Secret Garden   42

10 - A Vegan Considers Macbeth   45

11 - Three Times I Nearly Died   46

12 - Call Me Mr Snowman   51

13 - A Weekend in Wallop   53

14 - On Holiday with Brenda   57

15 - Winter, Tonbridge   60

16 - Another Show...   62

17 - Happiness   65

18 - Two Ladies at My Door   67

19 - Memorable Hotels   69

20 - A Grave on an Island   72

21 - How to Make Money from Diabetes   76

22 - And When I Watch the News   79

23 - Apology to the Archbishop   80

24 - My Dad's Capture   83

25 - Oh Yay, Oh Yay, Oh Yay   87

26 - Literally   90

27 - Empty Sunday   92

28 - Two Silly Men   95

29 - Advice to Young Comics   97

30 - Acceptance Speech   101

31 - Eighty-four   104

32 - Happiness Again   108

33 - Flying a Plane   111

34 - The Worst Entrance I Ever Made   114

35 - Eulogy for My English Teacher   117

36 - Spring   120

37 - A Brief Flutter   121

38 - Some Pleasures of Growing Old   123

39 - Socks in Art and Literature   125

40 - Reviewing the Sun and the Moon   **130**

41 - The Return of the Joke   **132**

42 - Middle of the Night   **135**

43 - Six Tiny Ways to Stave Off Misery   **136**

44 - Fish and Chips   **139**

45 - Arthur's Seat   **141**

46 - A Holiday Romance   **143**

47 - My Favourite Nuclear Bunker   **147**

48 - That's What He Would Have Wanted   **151**

49 - Mrs Burns and Quote Unquote   **152**

50 - Frisian Island Ferry Farce   **155**

51 - I Am a Late Worm   **157**

52 - Paris Poem   **159**

53 - Yoga with Goats   **162**

54 - On Being (a Wee Bit) Famous   **165**

55 - Once I...   **168**

56 - I Love Leonard Cohen   **170**

57 - The Old Wallonian Fourth Eleven   **174**

58 - To Wales then I Came   **177**

59 - Seated Badminton   **180**

60 - In Memoriam Dave   **182**

61 - Driving and Hitching   **184**

62 - Dealing with Derek the Bore   **189**

63 - Practical Jokes, Pranks, Hoaxes and April Fools   **191**

64 - Remembering Ned Sherrin   **195**

65 - My First Holiday   **198**

66 - How to Be a Caveman   **201**

67 - My Career in Politics   **204**

68 - Arty-ficial Intelligence   **208**

69 - In Praise of Plump   **210**

70 - Before the Exams   **212**

71 - Glasto Days   **214**

72 - Maybe It's Because I'm a South Londoner   **217**

73 - Elvis the Minicab Driver   **220**

74 - Rambling Man   **223**

75 - Anniversary   **226**

76 - Alpaca Trekking in Norfolk   **227**

77 - The Easiest Question I Ever Had to Answer   **230**

78 - Oscar and Gabby   **232**

79 - Dissing the Teletubbies   **236**

80 - Smoking   **238**

81 - The Oldest Cup in the Cupboard   **240**

82 - How to Be an Alternative Tour Guide   **242**

83 - PC Syd's Painful Night   **245**

84 - Losing It   248

85 - An Unusual Date   250

86 - Wrestling with Phones   253

87 - Art for Comedy's Sake   255

88 - Nearly 90   257

89 - Saturday in Athens   260

90 - Sleeping with Lord Nelson (and Others)   262

91 - Oh What a Day That Will Be   265

92 - The Sweetest Blackberries   267

93 - Travelling Man   270

94 - It's Late September   272

95 - Easy Smuggling   276

96 - And If By Chance   279

97 - Mindlessness   280

98 - Another Disaster That Didn't Happen   283

99 - I'm on the Train   285

100 - Flamingos in the Bar   286

Introduction

When an old person dies a library burns
to the ground
(African proverb)

Whoever you are, if you have been around on this earth for a while, you will have shelves full of memories and stories in your metaphorical library, a few of which may be worth telling.

Although I am not dead, one of the few things I am certain of is that someday I will be (for the PR people, ideally, just before this book is published) and therefore, before the flames of time destroy all record of my musings and adventures, I have curated a selection of them here for you. If you do not wince twice, gasp three times and laugh four times I shall be disappointed.

A good number of the *100 Things I Meant to Tell You* have taken place since the publication of my 2009 autobiography *My Name is Daphne Fairfax*, and although a few are very personal, most are pointing outwards at the ridiculous world we inhabit. It is a ragbag of escapades, a mosaic of anecdotage, a memoir in fragments, a parade of gags, speeches, poems, rants, obituaries, eulogies and baffled recollections.

Some of the pieces started life in public as articles in *The Guardian*, *The Stage* and *Woman's Weekly*, but I have changed and revisited them since then. I have also included three stories from my late father's memoir because they are more dramatic than anything I have lived through and because I would like my father's unique voice to be heard again.

Compared to most of the other seven billion people who hang out on the same planet as me I have been lucky in life. The two generations before me lived through World Wars; those that follow may face devastations that I can scarcely imagine. I have family, friends, a woman I love who loves me, and I have enjoyed working as a dustman, a writer, a broadcaster, a rock 'n roller, a warehouseman and a teacher – but mostly, I am pleased to say, as a comedian. You will find here a host of tales from the cackling caves of stand-up comedy.

Take your pick then, from my collection of ludicrous afternoons, dangerous days, disgraceful gigs, idle thoughts and exploits with friends… I am hoping that one of them may remind you of that hilarious thing that happened to you that time.

May I thank Donna Wood, my editor and sage advisor on this project who has chivvied and charmed and made all this possible. Also, my good friend Simon, who, along with Beth and the esteemed Mrs Charlton, has helped me sift through these memories.

And, as I usually say at the end of a show, 'Always remember the words of Lothian council – Tuesdays and Fridays are rubbish days.'

These fragments I have shored against my ruins
(T S Eliot, 'The Waste Land')

1

Grumpy Old Man

Grumpy Old Men was a celebrated 1993 American film starring Jack Lemmon and Walter Matthau. Ten years later the clever TV executive Stuart Prebble shamelessly stole the title for a BBC show that turned out to be a big success and remains the thing for which I am best known. I wondered at first why I had been asked to appear in it – I am probably no more grumpy than the next man – but the reaction to the series soon made me realise that the next man is *extremely* grumpy and the one next to him even grumpier.

So, one afternoon I sat on a bench outside a pub and spent an agreeable hour looking into a camera and railing at the world. I usually try not to be too cynical about the absurd business of being alive, but here I had licence to unleash every grouchy inner thought. I banged on about advertising, CCTV, rolling news, the etiquette of queuing, being 'kept on hold', young people (why can't I be one again?), bureaucrats, rogue apostrophes, celebrity culture, dog poo bags and anything else they wanted to cover. My cantankerous thesis became that the world was conspiring to sabotage the life of the Grumpy Old Man and keep him from his chosen pastime of sitting around in his underpants reading a book.

Me and my fellow 'talking heads' were glued together by Stuart's bilious script, which was delivered with masterful dry disdain by Geoffrey Palmer. Before the show aired, I expected any critical attention it drew would be unfavourable – who, after all, wants to watch old blokes peeving? And nobody likes to see ugly people clogging up airtime: 'Pack it in, Grandad, and get back to your shed.' Yet a chord was struck with the public, the show had good ratings, another series followed and then *Grumpy Old Women* proved equally popular.

Being negative has always been a mainstay of comedy; someone beamingly telling of their joy and happiness at their wonderful life may be inspiring for some, but it is never going to get many laughs. Another factor in the show's success was that it came at a time when everybody was now online and owned a mobile phone; the growing clamour of the outside world was becoming intolerable and my generation of 'techno immigrants' was appalled at having to be instantly contactable at all times. I still hanker after the days when, if you went on holiday for two weeks, nobody you knew had any idea, or any interest, in what you were up to or where you might be. I miss postcards.

Grumpy Old Men increased the number of seats I sold at one-man shows around the country and just before the interval I would invite the audience to write what they found annoying on a piece of paper, which I then read out in the second half. The winner was offered a weekend for two in a bedsit in Mitcham. There follows a selection of the best grumps I received and if you see that you wrote one of them I'll give you a free copy of this book and this time I won't renege on the Mitcham bedsit.

I'M GRUMPY BECAUSE
- I don't like the way my husband breathes.
- My partner is losing his hearing and can't hear me nagging him.
- When my girlfriend's coming up to her period we can only agree on one thing – we both wish *I* was dead.
- My son's going on a 'gap year'– gap from what?
- Pi doesn't equal 3.
- My wife is going through the menopause and has hot flushes, which means there is no heating on in the house and I am freezing. (Please do not reveal my name. She is with me but in the toilet as I write.)
- Since my dog died I can no longer pass my farts off as his.

Ironically, in the profoundly unlikely event of there being another series of *Grumpy Old Men*, I would be too old to take part. It should really have been called *Grumpy Middle-aged Men* because none of the contributors was yet eligible for the Senior Railcard, a fact which riled some older talking heads and especially the comic's comic, Barry Cryer.

Perhaps male grumpiness is the unacknowledged brother to the menopause and, in the end, they both pass. Certainly, I find now that while I can, at times, become anxious about the world and my place within it, I am also more accepting of the absurd deficiencies of life. As someone you can look up on Google once said, 'Infinite in his dreams but limited by his nature, man is a fallen angel who remembers heaven.'

2

How to Cope with Hecklers

Do you like to get drunk and abuse people? Then I propose you step away from Twitter and head to your nearest comedy club. Here you will find an arena where your desire to swear loudly at someone is acceptable and sometimes even encouraged.

Stand-up comedy is one of the few professions where attending to inebriate shouters is just another day at the office. They're paying you – why shouldn't they have a say, too? Heckling is not actually the same as trolling, since the heckler is there in the flesh (if not in full view) and may actually be trying to join in the occasion rather than scupper it. The comic should engage with them like a teacher with an unruly child, give them their moment but then take them down and bring the focus back to centre-stage. Occasionally the comic will fail. I still remember a woman who heckled me and my fellow Revue artists the first time we played in Wales. 'Why don't you all go back to London and leave us alone?' The sincerity in her voice floored us.

These days the punters at my shows tend to be older, more moderate souls, and my routines are rarely interrupted (other than by laughter, of course), but as the regular MC on weekends at the Comedy Store in Leicester Square in the 1980s, when the late show started at midnight and 'sobriety' was a word very few people present could pronounce, it was something I expected.

One way to disarm your enemy is to launch a stinging put-down that you have prepared in advance or stolen from another comic, such as:

'What a shame when cousins marry.'

'Yes, I remember when I had my first pint.'

'Nice to see the Bishop of Durham enjoying himself.'

Or Billy Connolly's memorable, 'Why don't you get yourself an agent instead of sitting there handling yourself in the dark?'

Sometimes you may have no answer worthy of the heckle. Not so long ago I was the compere at a comedy club in Ealing and there was a guy on who was even older than me. After five minutes he had barely raised a laugh. There was some uncomfortable shifting in the auditorium as yet another punchline sank into a lake of silence. Then, as he was about to deliver his next 'gag', a dismal clunker no doubt, a woman's voice rang out loudly and clearly.

'Excuse me – I think you really need to *think* about the way your life is going.'

She spoke with no trace of satire; rather, she had the concerned tone of a professional therapist who had spotted a man in need and was offering her services at a reduced rate. But the implication was obvious and devastating – not only is your act a disaster, so is your whole life. Even the world's quickest-ever comedian (Eric Morecambe, according to Barry Cryer) would have had a job stopping this bullet and the man on stage duly ground to a halt and shortly afterwards whispered goodnight.

He had left the building by the time I came off stage after introducing the next act. I have not seen him since.

A last resort in dealing with hecklers is to invite them to join you on stage. 'You think you're funny? Well, come up here and let's see how you do.' If they refuse this challenge then, game over, you have won. If they do stagger up, they are likely to find themselves disoriented and defeated by the bright lights shining in their eyes and the rows of people staring at them, awaiting their words.

Once, when I was MC at Jongleurs Comedy Club in Battersea, a bunch of guys on a stag night spent the entire evening heckling me and all the acts. I came on at the end to close the show and still they persisted. 'All right you lot,' I found myself saying, 'Why don't you come up and give us a goodnight song?'

'What shong?' slurred the chief stag, a miniature man in glasses with a preposterous bow-tie and a piercing voice. The audience laughed.

Now I was on the back foot and the air was filling with amused anticipation. 'Er...'

Come on, Arthur, think – quick! What's that silly single that's out?

'... What about *The Lion Sleeps Tonight*?'

Another big chuckle from the audience encouraged me to click my fingers and start the song. If you do not know *The Lion Sleeps Tonight*, I suggest you look at it on YouTube and imagine what followed.

'A-Wimoweh, A-Wimoweh, A-Wimoweh, A-Wimoweh...'

The men stood up and began to stumble their way onto the stage, whilst joining in with my 'Wimowehs' in an unexpectedly tuneful way. The lights seemed not to disturb them as they formed a perfect semicircle behind the small guy in the silly bow-tie, who duly stepped up to the microphone.

The next two and a half minutes was a sublime experience. The boozed-up stags sang with such vigour and beauty you would have thought they were all part of a professional choir – as I subsequently learned they were.

'In the jungle, the quiet jungle, the lion sleeps tonight...'

Small guy's counter tenor voice soared gloriously into that dark room. I stood at the side of the stage with my mouth open in wonder as I and the rest of the audience were blown away on a magic carpet of unexpected, tuneful pleasure. The night ended with a standing ovation. I hope the wedding went as well.

3

Walking into Gainsborough

The Romantic poets were the prototype ramblers and I've often found myself following in their footsteps – although perhaps not *all* of their footsteps, since a typical walk for Sam T Coleridge might last two days and cover 90 miles.

Coleridge, Wordsworth and their gang famously poeticised the Lake District, where the dramatic contours, jagged shadows and rocky terrain suited their temperaments, but they also roamed the West Country and the Downs of southeast England – Keats wrote 'Endymion' on Box Hill near Dorking. On the subject of the eastern hump of England, however, where there are no 'black chasms, and dizzy crags', the Romantics have nothing much to say.

Describing the Suffolk countryside demands a subdued vocabulary which is liable to include adjectives like 'subtle', 'gentle' and, of course, the controversial 'flat'. For a certain breed of rambler, 'flat' equals boring – a good view needs height just as a decent walk requires that you get out of puff struggling uphill. It is not surprising then that Suffolk and Norfolk rarely attract the attention of the striding wanderer.

But a day out in the delicate Suffolk folds, I have learned, can, if you are too complacent, be as demanding as a march up a sweaty northern mountain; the only one of all my walks where I needed the attentions of a rescuer with a big torch was in Walberswick in Suffolk when it got dark before I could find a path out of the marshy reeds.

Nevertheless, unless you become even more lost and late than usual, you are unlikely to need the phone number of the Suffolk Mountain Rescue team. The undulations of the land are not as physically demanding or attention-seeking as those of Cumbria, but this is the corner of England which, half a century before the Romantics, inspired works by Constable and Gainsborough, two of the best loved among English landscape painters.

The train from Marks Tey taking you east canters along the leafy Stour Valley and passes over the mighty Chappel Viaduct before arriving in Sudbury. The Gainsborough line, as this part of the railway network is called, is a tribute to the little town's most famous ex-resident and, after a bossily signposted mile or so, I was soon marching past ponds and along paths which looked familiar from the jigsaws and biscuit tins of my childhood. Gainsborough and Constable have shifted a heap of merchandise over the years.

You get a lot of sky for your money in these parts and sky is a big challenge for all artists. In the book I bought about Gainsborough, Hugh Belsey writes of *Wooded Landscape with Herdsman Seated*, 'the effect of the painting depends on the tranquil cloudscape that mottles the landscape beneath with pools of sunlight'. But also, the Herdsman is wearing a little straw hat like mine.

Sky and clouds and trees and little figures relaxing in the perfect rural rhythm of their surroundings: these are the staples of a Gainsborough landscape. After four miles I, too, sat under a tree like the Herdsman and let the minimalism of my surroundings slow my mind. I remembered my days as a cross-country runner in Norfolk and the punishing effort of traversing huge, wet, ploughed-up fields, and then I sat some more. Although there are fewer herdsmen, peasants, milkmaids and packhorses than in Gainsborough's day, the subtle curves of the land and the angular trees of his images are still in evidence. The titles of his paintings and sketches serve as a description of what you see on an amble through Suffolk.

Landscape with Figures, Cottages and Cow

Study of a Wooded Landscape with Country Lane

A Pathway through a Landscape with a Farm in
   the Distance

'The landscape of Gainsborough', wrote Constable, 'is soothing, tender and affecting', and so was this walk, which I rounded off with a tour of the Gainsborough museum, a large, elegant house in Sudbury that contains all the pictures mentioned above, as well as copies of the Belsey book. You can indulge in a little 18th-century tour or look at one of the contemporary exhibitions the museum also mounts. I was welcomed grandly to the house by a charming and formidable trio of ladies, one of whom will dress up as Mrs Gainsborough if you ask her nicely.

I took a look round the pretty garden and its 200-year-old mulberry tree, which resembles a huge, grounded octopus, and then sipped a cup of tea, enjoyed the touch of weariness in my legs and dreamed a gentle pastoral dream that was suffused by Suffolk.

4

Ken and Doug

As you walk to Balham tube station in the early morning, you often see Ken clutching a can of Special Brew, waving his arms like an Italian, and enthusiastically singing what might once have been an aria.

Ken, our most prominent drunk, is as much a part of the local community as Reita in the laundrette, the local mums pushing prams or Lucia from the Italian – in fact *more* so, since he is highly visible, enormously voluble and endlessly entertaining. Everyone knows Ken. Apart from light opera, he loves to dispense philosophy and advice to all who pass. It is rarely possible to identify any actual words in his pronouncements but, no matter, his general drift is clear and consistently upbeat.

He may be bald but Ken sports a raggedy beard which is soaked in strong lager and studded with mysterious morsels; in my opinion it should be declared a Site of Special Scientific Interest. He emanates a ripe urban aroma, while his clothes are wildly various – one day he may be wearing an ancient thin, filthy jumper, the next his scraggy torso is housed in an enormous padded ski-ing jacket. I think he sleeps in the small hostel by the church.

Ken's favoured spot is the bench on the pavement outside the Wetherspoon's pub, where he is usually to be found with his sidekick Doug, a huge, jowly man whose deep, hushed monologues provide a perfect bass line to Ken's strident tones. Neither of them ever goes into the pub, preferring to bring their own cans, but they are friends with all the boozers who come outside for a smoke.

Doug, who must live somewhere nearby, is a creature of habit. He shuffles along Balham High Road each morning at around 11am, wearing trousers that are nearly up to his neck, his white plastic bag of booze grasped in an enormous red fist. He leans heavily on his stick and pauses every 20 yards for a rest against a wall. His progress is slow and sweaty but his determination is inspiring. On arrival at Ken's bench he sinks into its welcoming wooden arms and pants heavily for several minutes before embarking on another day of muttering and sipping. Ken punches Doug's arm affectionately as they clink cans and cackle together.

I do not know how the lads came to lead these lives but they show no signs of wanting to change them. Sometimes, it is hard not to conclude that they are, in many ways, happier than we inhabitants of the conventional world with our frenetic worries. But perhaps I am thinking that because, of course, I used to drink myself...

As the day wears on, Ken's rhetoric and Doug's minimalist chatter become more animated until they reach a crescendo of brotherhood. Not long after this, especially if the day is warm, stressed commuters coming home from work are likely to see the pair of them blissfully conked out on the bench, snoring their way into the early evening. And I don't doubt that, like me, they are reassured that all is well in Balham town.

5

Eighty

Walking through Soho on my way to Charing Cross, as I seem to do weekly now, I note a long queue of people outside what I presume must be the venue for some afternoon concert, but it turns out to be a fancy dress shop. Tomorrow is Hallowe'en, an occasion whose observation has grown as Guy Fawkes' has declined. Tomorrow is also my mother Hazel's 80th birthday and tonight I will stay with her in Tonbridge, where my younger brother Nick lives. She moved there after my dad Syd died so she could help with Nick and Sue's three boys.

Arriving at Tonbridge station I ring Mum so she can walk down the hill to meet me coming up. It is her favourite thing. Usually, soon after my call, her tiny grey head comes into view, she waves her stick in greeting and I put down my bags of shopping and wave back. But not today.

The person you are calling is not available. Please leave a message after the tone.

When she goes to bed she places a stick against the inside of the front door. It clatters to the floor as I let myself in and turn the light on. 'Hello Mother,' I whisper loudly. When I get upstairs to her bedroom she has woken up. 'Hello, dear boy!'

She eats some of the prawn sandwich I have brought, though not much of the salad, and knocks back half a bottle of wine.

'How are you and your people?' This is a familiar question.

'What time is it? Is it evening or morning?' 'Ah, let's put the six o'clock news on.'

'Have you had enough to eat?' Another of her regular questions.

'How are you and your people?'

'Can I get you anything? Have you had enough to eat?'

We go out to sit on the bench in her garden and look up at the flashing lights of the traffic going in and out of Gatwick.

'I'm glad I don't have to go in planes anymore.'

'Well, that's a shame because I've got us tickets to fly to China, leaving in 10 minutes.'

'Oh, dear boy,' she gasps at the thought but she knows I am joking as, despite it all, she always does. 'No, I'd like to stay here. Have you had enough to eat?'

'But we're going out clubbing shortly, Mother.' She laughs again and soon she totters off back to bed. I allow her time for a pee then go up to kiss her goodnight. I return to the bench and look at the dark sky punctured by the neon of the lamp post in the alley at the back of the garden.

Next morning, she makes me a cup of tea and wants a bath. 'Eighty!' she exclaims. 'How ridiculous, how terrible.' After I have helped her in and out of the bath, I make her a piece of toast and produce another bottle of white wine.

As she drinks, she has the second half of yesterday's prawn sandwich. She takes a couple of phone calls from well-wishers but the bottle is finished now and I persuade her to have another sleep before her birthday lunch with her sons.

Richard, having been at some medical conference, arrives direct from Frankfurt via Heathrow in a cab. Mother and I join him and the three of us soon enter the country pub where Nick is waiting. When were we four last all together? Was it Dad's funeral? It is clear Hazel has little appetite and as we eat our starters, she drains her wine and announces she is going back up to bed again.

'Not yet, Mother, we're in a pub.'

'Oh.' She looks crestfallen and then blank. We three brothers chat on but Hazel will not be drawn in.

'I think I'll go and have a little lie down.'

We skip pudding and get a taxi back to her house. She revives a little when Nick's boys come round. 'Lovely little fellas.' She receives some presents.

'Soap,' says little Jack. 'Old people always get that as a present.'

Richard and I walk down the hill back to the station. On the train we discuss her worsening dementia and how much longer she can stay like this. Where shall we put her? As I walk along the road home I ring her. Nick, Sue and the boys will have left by now.

The person you are calling is not available. Please leave a message after the tone.

Around me, excited girls dressed as vampires are setting off for a big night out.

6

If

(by Arthur Kipling)

If you can roll along at a decent pace,
And you find that your rear contains
   lots of space,
If you have windows at the front yet none
   at the side,
And offer a smooth, unflashy ride,
If you have a red and white flag on your bonnet
And could never imagine doing a ton,
Then yours is the road and everything on it,
And, which is more, you'll be a van my son.

7

Passenger Announcement

The train taking me to Nantwich grinds to a halt in a tunnel outside the station. It is hot and crowded and we passengers, or, as we are now known, 'customers', are sweating and exasperated. There is a bing-bong and then the following announcement. 'Good afternoon, this is your driver speaking. I'm sorry for the delay. This is due to the fat greedy gits who own this company.'

Passengers exchange smirks.

'All they care about is money – they're not bothered about your pathetic trip to Nantwich. Where is Nantwich anyway? I don't know and I'm the driver of the train.'

Now, despite the stuffiness and discomfort, people are giggling – an exceedingly rare occurrence on a British train. She continues, 'Or rather I *was* the driver of the train – you may take this as my resignation.' Loud hoots of merriment reverberate between the carriages. 'And while I've got your attention I'd like to tell you about some trouble I've been having with my husband... 25 happy years – and then we met each other.'

Everyone is laughing as the driver continues with a stream of ripe old gags and, in true showbiz style, closes with a spirited rendition of The Monkees' great hit, *Last Train to Clarksville*, substituting, of course, 'Nantwich' for 'Clarksville.'

When we finally crawl into the station we have been united by one person and we all have a tale to tell. That woman was a hero, or rather she *would* have been one had she truly existed instead of being a character I dreamed up to demonstrate my theory about the healing power of laughter. It's true though, isn't it? On the rare occasions when a train driver departs from her (or his) script and makes a witticism that shows their humanity, there is an instant bond created between the passengers sharing the moment.

My old routine came back to me when I agreed to participate in a scheme aimed at tube drivers on the Piccadilly line of the London Underground. They were each given a booklet containing weighty or humorous quotations selected by the artist Jeremy Deller, a unique and original creator who pays the public the tribute of *looking* like an artist. My job was to do a turn for the drivers, encouraging them to read some of these quotes out over the PA to supplement the normal diet of obligatory and superfluous phrases. For example, 'As one gets older, one discovers everything is going to be exactly the same with different hats on. Change here for the Hammersmith and City line.' Or, 'He who digs a pit for another will fall into it himself. Mind the gap.'

I was really hoping I could pull this off so that I could have a hand in resisting the impersonal and ever-multiplying announcements that anyone who uses public transport is obliged to hear. 'Smoking is not permitted anywhere on this train.' Really? When did that happen? I never knew. The example I find most insidious and depressing is 'If you see anything suspicious please report it to a member of staff.' I don't know why they don't just say, 'See that bloke opposite? I bet he's an evil bastard.' Lately we London tubers have learned to restrain ourselves from screaming as yet again we are advised to 'See it, say it – sorted', or as I render it, 'See it, soddit, leave it.'

If the scheme had gone well there were plans to extend it to other underground lines but, alas, since my gig I have never heard a quote from Plato as I stood on the Northern line in the rush hour with a stranger's head up my jumper. I think it felt too weird for the drivers to start delivering lines from the solitude of their cabin at the front. Besides, they are tube drivers, not public speakers. Oh well, can't win 'em all – go for bronze.

That is the end of this thing I meant to tell you. Please remember to take all your possessions when leaving the page. And remember too – 'Laughter is the one true metaphysical consolation', as Nietzsche nearly said.

8

The Joy of Not Going

I remember Denise's 60th. I really enjoyed that day. I didn't expect to, because Denise now lives in some distant Scottish village and we'd grown apart in recent years – especially since she had chosen to marry a man who was dull when sober, obnoxious when drunk and unavoidable if you were both in the same building. And then there was her long-winded brother, a man capable of speaking for hours about nothing in particular, without ever apparently finishing a sentence. But it was Denise's special birthday, she'd been a very good friend to me over the years and I was due to give a speech; I HAD to go.

Mind you, I was dreading the journey – hours and hours, taking up most of Friday to be there ready for the party on the Saturday – if you added it up, a whole weekend of my life when I had an article to write that could not wait until Monday. Perhaps I could do a bit on the train? Which reminds me – dear God, the cost of the train ticket! For what? Being sober while both the husband and brother were drunk.

But, as it turned out, I had a splendid weekend because just as I was about to set off on my interminable journey, Denise rang to say that her husband had come down with the flu and the whole thing was off!

Choirs crescendoed! The weekend rolled out in front of me like a vast, beautiful lawn and I experienced a surge of joy that I am sure no drug could ever provide. It started raining outside as I kicked my shoes off, put my pyjama bottoms on, ordered some takeaway pizza and settled down to watch the last four episodes of that Scandinavian drama to which Beth and I had both become addicted. I now decided my article could wait until Monday – easily – yeeeahhhh… Hey, this was pretty close to bliss!

In my 20s, of course, I went to parties all the time. Most nights I was out in pursuit of love, excitement, drama, drink and comedy. It helped that the slum I shared with three other reprobates was so scruffy and cold that a cosy night in was not possible. Now that I am older, no longer drink alcohol, have Beth, a comfortable home and a top-class pair of slippers, my gallivanting is no more; you can't read a novel in a nightclub. I am turning into Dr Johnson, who once memorably described a play as, 'worth seeing – but not worth *going* to see.'

You cannot expect the ecstasy of cancellation every time and you shouldn't abandon all social and cultural events but I propose you only show up to the ones you might actually *enjoy*. Even so, a time will come when you find you have agreed to go to a dinner party where three of the guests are Scientologists, or to a six-hour experimental opera written by the friend of a friend.

Now is the time! Take a big breath, buff up your best excuse and make that call. It may prove a prickly conversation but it will only last a minute or two and then, oh most wonderful, you can change into your slobbiest clothes, make a nice cup of tea and consider all the options that have suddenly opened up before you.

9

Secret Garden

Beth and I live in a building seven floors high which has a small secret garden round the back by the garages and the skip, where the foxes slink by after their heavy nights out on the town. Tended by volunteer residents and with a small wooden bench, this tiny, flowery place with its hidden entrance is always deserted at night, when I occasionally go and sit there to gaze up at all the windows and imagine all those other lives.

One warm night not long after I moved here I was joined in my little hermitage by my pal Tony Hawks and this was where we invented a game called Secret Garden. Slow-moving and completely unpredictable, it can be played for 10 minutes or 10 hours. You don't actually need a garden, but you do need to be looking at a tall building or house, preferably just as evening is closing in. (NB You should be far enough away to differentiate you from a Peeping Tom.)

Each player is allotted a line of windows, depending on how tall the building is – in Du Cane Court I traditionally take the top three rows, and Beth, who is now my regular opponent, takes the three underneath. This is the 'board' on which the game is to be played, and you are now on START. Assess your own lines, and those of your opponent. Some of these windows will be dark, some will have lights on, some of the curtains will be drawn, some will be open. Keep looking at the windows…

Points are awarded for any change. If a light comes on or goes off in one of your rows, if a person appears, or if the curtains are pulled back, you get one point for each. Multiple points can come in a burst. For example, a man comes home from work and:

1) Puts the light on
2) Appears at the window
3) Draws the curtains
4) Appears at his adjacent bathroom
5) Turns the light on there
6) Appears at the window washing his hands
7) Turns it off again
8) Comes back
9) Opens the window – leans out (possibly in the distance he sees two tiny players sitting on a bench)

Although these are all the same person in the same house, they are separate points: nine in all. There are no real tactics other than a keen pair of eyes – as in life, much of your success is down to luck. But as you play, you will find the conversation flows easier than if you are just sitting there waiting to say something. Or if you long for silence, she will grace you with her peace, interspersed only by a blurted claim for points: 'Man at window row 2!'

It was during a game of Secret Garden that I first asked Beth to call me by the name I am known by to my family and old friends – Brian, not Arthur – and my rather shy and formal way of doing so was absorbed by the lines of windows at which we stared. A month later, we bonded deeply following the most sensational event ever to occur during a game of Secret Garden: the woman with the dimmer switch.

She lives on the second-from-bottom floor at the far right-hand side as you look at it – Beth's row – but hey, I was leading 5-0 at the time. The woman appeared at the window and looked out (1 point) then went and switched on the light (2 points). Now the action really heated up: she brightened the light (3 points); took it down again (4 points); came to the window again (5 points); went back to the dimmer and lowered it still further (6 points). That was it, surely? No, she came back again, and in a final, sensational flourish, adjusted the dimmer to a comforting, just-right yellow glow (7 points). Defeated – game to Beth.

Two years later, when I returned home after learning my father had terminal cancer, we played a silent, rather comforting game as I tried to gather my strength for the sadness that awaited. It was a form of meditation that night.

Perhaps I could market Secret Garden as a profound new kind of therapy that relaxes all your despair away? Turn myself into a wellness billionaire? I don't think so, but feel free to give the game a try yourself.

10

A Vegan Considers Macbeth

Tomorrow, and to marrow, and tomato,
Crêpes in this petit pois from date to date,
To the last cinnamon of acorn in thyme,
Tandoori yeasterdays have lighted gruels,
The waiter crusty bread. Sprout, sprout,
   leaf canderel!
Life's but a portion of Tabasco, a red pepper
That nuts courgettes its flour upon the sage,
And then is stirred no more. It is some kale
Rolled in a vinaigrette, full of ground-up purée
Signifrying muffin.

11

Three Times I Nearly Died

1. It's 1977 and I am in Norwich taking part in the University of East Anglia freshers' week. I have just left home and am going to have to learn at least a few of the skills you need to call yourself an adult. So far, so good; I have unpacked, said hello to my new room-mate and managed to make myself sausage and mash, as detailed in Katharine Whitehorn's legendary student bible, *Cooking in a Bedsitter*, a parting gift from my mother. Now I am in the Student Union bar with an assortment of fellow freshers, among whom is Angie, the first public-school girl I have ever met. She has a posh accent like you hear on the BBC and, even rarer among my contemporaries, she owns a car! Yes, it is only a Mini but how can an 18-year-old afford a car? Soon we are all discussing one of the great topics of the age: 'How many people can you fit in a Mini?'

A couple of hours and several pints later, a dozen or so of us decide to answer this question and stagger out to the road leading to the campus. Angie pulls up in her car and students start piling in. After a deal of grunting, squealing and squeezing, the Mini is squashed full of distorted bodies, leaving six would-be record breakers still without a place. No problem – three climb onto the roof and I take my place between Jenny and Laura on the bonnet.

Angie, who has drunk a truly impressive quantity of white wine, throws her arms around the two bodies on her lap, takes the wheel, sticks her head out of the car window and sets off, driving slowly. We all hoot in delight at this marvellous, friend-making game. She begins to speed up and my chortling subsides as I feel my bottom slowly inching down the bonnet towards the road. Now she accelerates to what I later guess to be 40mph and the street moving so quickly beneath me is getting closer and closer.

Jenny and Laura are each clinging onto a wing mirror and screaming. I am clinging onto nothing and also screaming. What can I do? If I grab my fellow bonneteers, might we all three fall in front of the speeding car? I am looking death in the face and I don't like him at all. 'Stop! Stop!' Everyone on the outside is shouting and, thank God, just before my legs are crunched beneath the number plate, Angie slows and we finally come to a halt. I am shocked and suddenly very sober. We probably didn't beat the record for most people in (and on) a Mini but we came very close to 'most freshers killed in a car crash on their first night at university.'

2. As an undergraduate I became a devoted fan of one of the great poets of our age, the late Leonard Cohen, and years later I wrote a show in which I sang some of his songs.

Learning lines takes a lot of concentration and one day in early summer, a week before my first performance of the Leonard show, I spent an afternoon going through the words and song lyrics in my head while listening to the backing tracks on my iPod. I chose to do this sitting on the empty slice of scruffy Thames beach that lies beneath the Oxo Tower on the South Bank. I shut my eyes and focused, muttering the words and singing the songs over and over...

My concentration was suddenly shattered by the sound of whooshing water. Opening my eyes, I saw that the river's water level was rising and I remembered the Thames is tidal. I grabbed my stuff and stood up sharply to walk the 10 yards to the stairway that led up to safety but then the water surged forward several feet more and now the bottom steps were submerged so that I could only reach them if I *waded* there. Uh-oh. I'm in trouble here.

I looked at the wall against which I had been sitting. Could I climb it and haul myself over the railings? No, it was too high, with no protuberances that might serve as handles. Another gurgle and the water hit the wall on either side of me. Now the only way to the steps was to swim. There was only about a square yard of sand left to stand on. I grabbed my phone from my pocket and rang 999.

As I waited anxiously, water lapped at my feet and I braced myself. For a moment I was both appalled and amused at the thought that I was going to share a 'cause of death' with my old friend and fellow comic Malcolm Hardee, who drowned one drunken night in the Thames further down river.

And then suddenly I was flooded, not with water but with relief, at the sight of a boat approaching my tiny island. I waved my arms more vigorously than ever before. 'Over here!' Hoorah for the Thames Water Police! They hauled me aboard, ascertained that I was not drunk or up to no good, gave me a telling-off, laughed and let me go at Waterloo pier.

3. My own foolishness caused the first two near-deaths but the third time I nearly didn't make it was not down to me but to the hormones that flow through cows just after they have given birth. I warn you – beware cows in May.

Two of them were sitting languidly chewing the cud and nestling their calves in the field through which I and my fellow ramblers were walking that spring day in the Peak District. We had heard about angry cows but they showed no interest in our passing until they spotted Django, the dog on the lead held by Ralph, the rambler bringing up our rear. Seeing Django, the cows got angrily to their feet and stared at him aggressively.

Sensing, correctly, that the cows hated the dog more than any of us, Ralph let go of the lead and Django went sprinting down the slope with the cows in hot, grunting pursuit. My fellow walkers scattered but I was at the bottom of the hill looking back up at the cows stampeding down towards me. There was no time to run. Django flew past me and, in a second, I was confronted by an image that is emblazoned in my memory like no other. Like some epic oil painting, two huge jowly animals, massive teeth bared, fill the frame, their eyes wild with fury, five feet away, heading straight at me. Was this the last thing I would ever see?

Well, obviously not. At the last moment the cows separated and ran either side of my frozen body, missing me by a whisker, as they continued their pursuit of the offending dog. Django leapt over a wall, as we all did, and my terror merged into the astounded, relieved laughter of my friends. Later, in the pub, one of them spotted an article in the local paper about a rambler who had been crushed to death by cows the week before.

Once again I enjoyed the brief ecstasy that comes from not dying when you thought you were going to; it's a formidable feeling but not one I suggest you seek out. But should you at any time wish to put some perspective on your anxieties, remember that occasion where, if things had happened only *slightly* differently, you might not be alive to read this. And be thankful.

12

Call Me Mr Snowman

For four years, while I tried to break into show business in the evenings, I spent my weekdays teaching English to foreign students in North London, a rewarding job which provided frequent insights into the state that so many Brexiteers disapprove of – not being British. I also learned that dismantling your maternal language can prove a useful prelude to reassembling it in an interesting way.

One morning, as I was pontificating on the difference between the present continuous tense and the present simple, the class was distracted by the sight of snow falling fluffily outside. 'Sometimes it snows and now it is snowing'. I tried to incorporate this topical event into my explanation but it was apparent I had lost my audience. Hassan, a student from Iran, gasped in awe as he stared through the window: 'I never see snow!'

'I think, Hassan, you mean, *I have never seen snow.* That's the present perfect. Has anyone else never seen snow?' I enquired, employing the present perfect interrogative. Mansoor from Iraq and Anita from Nigeria raised their hands, their heads swivelled away from me so as not to miss a moment of this astounding event, at which point I realised that the formal element of this lesson was over.

We all bundled out to the garden opposite the language school, where the grass was gently turning white in a most inviting way. I watched the three snow virgins as they roared their laughs into the frozen air like excited children who had just been given a really great birthday present. They fondled in slushy ecstasy the first snowflakes they had ever seen and launched their first snowballs at the other students.

It was a memorable morning and the pleasure I took from the students' undisguised delight was augmented by the respect I was accorded because, of course, as the teacher, I was somehow *responsible* for the snow turning up like this. For the rest of that term I was known as 'Mr Snowman'. One day, maybe, I will experience the same elemental stimulation if I ever get to see the Northern Lights. Hope so.

13

A Weekend in Wallop

'Phil! Did you have to ring me so early?'

'It's four o'clock in the afternoon, Arthur. Listen, do you want to do a gig on Friday in a place called Nether Wallop for no fee?'

'God no. Where's Nether Wallop anyway?'

At this time in the early 1980s I was in a double act called Fiasco Job Job with my old pal Phil Nice. We had two Edinburgh shows under our belts and were doing well on the comedy circuit, well enough not to need to travel to somewhere with what seemed like a made-up name to do a show for no money. I am glad, however, that Phil persuaded me to go because if he had not, I would have missed one of the most entertaining weekends of my life.

This unlikely festival came about because of a remark tossed off by critic Stephen Pile in an article asking why the Edinburgh Festival had to happen in Edinburgh. Why couldn't it be held in somewhere like, say, Nether Wallop? Paul Jackson, then a big cheese at London Weekend Television and the man responsible for *The Young Ones*, was clearly tickled by this idea and proceeded to concoct an extraordinary weekend event featuring an astonishing array of talent. Nether Wallop lies in rural Hampshire close to its fellow Wallops – Over Wallop and Middle Wallop. The place had a comic name and, Paul reasoned, deserved a charity comedy festival which could also be made into a TV show.

Phil and I were invited along to do a turn on the Friday night, representing the Fringe. We duly turned up to find that our venue was the Scout hut and we were sharing a bill with names far bigger than ours, including actor Sir Michael Hordern, two of my heroes – the Liverpool poets Roger McGough and Brian Patten – and, closing the show, the local vicar doing his magic act with the sublime Jenny Agutter as his glamorous assistant.

After our set Phil had to return home but, having blagged a hotel on LWT, I chose to stick around for the weekend to enjoy the wondrous range of happenings on offer in this normally sleepy hamlet. These included a performance by the local Brownie troop choreographed by Wayne Sleep; Ned Sherrin and Gore Vidal in the village shop; and a live version of *University Challenge* in which its then host, Bamber Gascoigne, pitted a team of farmers against a team of top academics including the philosopher A J Ayer. Many of the questions were about farming and the locals won. Sometime in the afternoon I and my fellow comic Norman Lovett did a spot on the back of a lorry trailer to a herd of unappreciative cows.

On the Sunday I managed to wangle myself a tiny spot on the bill for the big gig in a large tent, pitched on a nearby field. It was MC-ed by a local dignitary and performers included Rowan Atkinson; Mel Smith and

Peter Cook (as two members of a lesbian synchronised swimming team); Hugh Laurie; Stephen Fry; Rik Mayall first as 'Kevin Turvey' and then later singing *Trouble* with Jools Holland on piano and Bill Wyman on guitar. A stellar line-up no doubt, but it seems shocking to me now to see a bill featuring not one woman.

Top of the bill, and correctly so, was the incomparably gifted Billy Connolly, who, as ever, thrilled the large crowd with his improvisatory brilliance. And I should like to take this opportunity to apologise to the great man, because afterwards there was a big party where I somehow ended up asking him 'Why do you send your kids to public school?' as though *I* should be the one to decide on his children's education. I wince to remember this. Connolly was understandably furious at me.

'You don't know what it's like being famous!' He jabbed his finger at me and told me I was shit in my spot in the show, to which I responded, 'Well, I was only on for 10 seconds.'

'Yes, that's you,' he spat. 'You're a 10-second comedian.'

Following this withering put-down I stepped back from the fray. There is no doubt that, compared to Billy Connolly, I am indeed a 10-second comedian.

I ended that evening flipping coins with fellow boozers Peter Cook and Mel Smith for a tenner a time, which left me penniless and meant I had to hitch-hike home the next day. When I got a lift I babbled excitedly to the driver about all the famous people I had met over the weekend. The man, who was not a local and knew nothing of the festival, was clearly not convinced that such a glamorous gathering had occurred in this rural backwater and perhaps imagined I was a deluded fantasist. I changed the subject to reassure him and wrapped up my memories for inspection here 35 years later.

14

On Holiday with Brenda

There is really only one way to guarantee you will enjoy a holiday and that is to make sure that you have Brenda Kilcoyne with you. Brenda is Beth's mum and when Beth and I finally manage to organise our wedding, Brenda will officially become my mother-in-law and all will be right with the world.

Brenda and John, both retired teachers, live in Sunderland, where Beth and her sister Emma were raised, but they are originally from Keighley in Yorkshire. John has a gag, which I have brazenly stolen: 'A Yorkshireman is like a Scotsman with all the generosity squeezed out of him.' This always raises a laugh but it is not appropriate to John and Brenda, who, ever since I met them, have shown a kindness and generosity that make a visit to Sunderland a guaranteed restful delight.

Not long after Beth and I moved in together I was invited to take part in an event at the British Embassy in Paris to mark 100 years of the exchange scheme that allowed me to spend a year in France as an English assistant. I managed to wangle tickets for Beth and Brenda, and this is when I first learned that Brenda's enthusiasm and interest in every detail of a trip abroad are superbly infectious.

She marvelled at our elegant hotel near the Eiffel Tower, she loved meeting the British Ambassador, Sir John Holmes, and was fascinated by the canapés, the cake and the various dignitaries we encountered. Seeing her and Beth beaming supportively at me from the front row at the Embassy supplied an added warmth to my speech about my Parisian days.

A couple of years later Brenda and John came with me and Beth to Switzerland, where I was booked for some shows, and the Swiss Alps put on an especially great show to impress Brenda. We were given a tour of CERN, the home of the Hadron Collider, which was especially fascinating to John, who had been the top chemistry lecturer at Sunderland University. We were all supplied with white coats to wear for our visit but Brenda's heels were not permitted so she was given a pair of flat shoes that were much too big for her. John explained to me the significance of the place but my abiding memory of CERN will always be Brenda smiling in her white coat and clown shoes.

And then there was Rome. Brenda is a devout Catholic (one of the nice ones), whose appreciation of St Cuthbert is second to none, so Beth and I were thrilled to accompany her and John on their first visit to the Eternal City. We arrived at night and checked into the hotel I had carefully chosen. After breakfast next morning I led us all on a short walk.

I knew, though Brenda didn't, what we would see in front of us once we had passed through those dark Bernini columns and I could hardly wait to register

Brenda's reaction. As we came into the light, there it stood in all its magnificence: St Peter's Basilica, mother church of Catholicism. Brenda gazed at the great dome in wonder for a second, clasped her hands together and fell to her knees weeping.

And unexpectedly, so did I.

Always take Brenda when you go abroad.

15

Winter, Tonbridge

One night I got a phone call from my mother's neighbours describing the incident in this poem. Distressing though it was, it confirmed our need to do something to make her safe.

Pulling up late
After the party,
They see her,
Their neighbour,
Standing in the street.

She is looking, she says,
For a lift to London.
She needs to get home
To London.
'Hazel,' they tell her,
'This is your home,
You live here in this house.
London is 30 miles away.'

Her door is open.
They take her in
And see she has packed a bag
(If a jumper and a biscuit count as packing.)

Oh Hazel,
It is 35 years since you left London
To live, as you liked to say, 'in the shires'.
But there she still is,
The grammar school girl
From Camberwell Green,
Dancing, kissing sailors
In Trafalgar Square.

It is VE day
And the rest
Of the century
Is yours.

16

Another Show...

It is shiveringly cold at Paddington station when I board the 13.22 to Taunton but the train warms me and, hey, come on, you're working Arthur, I elect to pay the £20 weekend supplement to upgrade to first class. I sink down and replace my outdoor shoes with the slippers I always wear for any journey of more than two hours.

From my window seat I gaze into the frozen landscape, as ever imagining myself within it in my walking boots with a map and a warm jacket. I go over some routines in my head and make notes towards this forthcoming performance. On arrival at Taunton, I check in to my rather grand hotel and walk the empty Sunday streets in search of a local paper that might furnish me with a gag or two about the town. I fail to find one.

At the venue, The Brewhouse, I am politely welcomed by the charming technicians whom I shall call Karen and Bob. We swiftly organise my minimal lighting and sound cues before I alert them that my stage time is about the same as Ken Dodd's (Doddie was a great comic who loved being in front of an audience more, I suspect, than anything else in his life; his show, which might last as long as a Wagner opera, delighted audiences but oppressed the backstage crew for whom it meant hours of unpaid overtime). A nanosecond of shock registers on the faces of Karen and Bob before they smile politely.

'And have you,' I continue, 'arranged the lasers and the stairs that light up as I come down for my big entrance?'

'Yes,' says Karen. 'And the roof opens up as well.'

It transpires that Bob has a copy of the local paper. I take it to my dressing room and they 'open the house'.

As the audience starts to arrive I alternate pacing around backstage with smoking fags outside the back door by the bins until it is time to go on. Standing in the wings I make the announcement, 'Ladies and gentlemen, please welcome...', the lights go down, I take a big breath, 'Me!' I walk to the mic at centre stage.

The crowd, a decent 250 plus, is friendly and appreciative. After some scripted grumpy grumbling, I read out the story of the Taunton man who got trapped under his sofa for three days and survived by drinking whisky. I hardly need to add anything to get laughs. I improvise a routine about my train journey down, and how inappropriate the name First Great Western is, suggesting they should change it to 'Seventh Crap Western'. My rude remarks about rival local town Bridgwater do better.

All goes well. Afterwards, since the theatre bar is closed and I don't have anyone to meet, I escape out of the stage door, having bid farewell to Karen and Bob.

As I walk along by a dark, frozen riverbank to my hotel, I relish the contrast between the loud, illuminated noise of the thing I just did and the indifferent silence of the arctic night through which I now move.

In my room I have a shower, ring Beth, order a sandwich on room service then sit and watch a TV show about a man and some bears in Alaska or somewhere. It gently saps my adrenaline until I am almost ready for sleep. A last smoke outside, a chat with the night porter and so to bed.

Next morning I indulge myself with porridge and a large fry-up while reading a novel by J G Ballard. Comedians don't do Monday mornings. Through a glass door I can see business people in suits and heels and ties having a meeting; thank goodness I am not one of them.

Since there have been heavy snowfalls further east I am expecting some trouble with the trains. At the station a member of staff at First Great Western tells me he was at the gig last night but he is smiling rather than upset about the jokes. Amazingly, the train leaves, and arrives, on time. Once in London I get on the tube, which despite my fears, runs perfectly. I arrive home, where Beth greets me in our warm, cosy flat.

It has not been an exceptional gig. It's just one among hundreds I have done on my various tours around Britain. I blow into town with my overnight bag, do my dance and go. It's just another day at the coal face of comedy, a day like any other job, except I earned more in that evening than a nurse does in a week.

I thank my lucky stars once more for the privileged position in which I find myself: a well-paid, wandering troubadour singing my song to the inhabitants of one clearing and then moving on to the next.

17

Happiness

It is the early 1990s and on the soft beach of the small Cornish cove, drying off after my spontaneous leap into the sea, I sit with my back to a rock, light a cigarette and have a very unusual thought: 'Gosh, I am happy.'

I have walked an exhilarating 10 miles up and down the fierce contours of the coastline and now, ahead of me, I have a gentle two-mile stroll to my clifftop hotel. I am looking forward to a bath with the intensity that can come only from a long, active, sweaty day in the sun.

All this is pleasing, but the main catalyst for my good mood is that I have an assignation: a woman is driving down from London to meet me later this evening in my seaside palace on the cliffs. I do not know her very well but we have shared one – sensational – date. My room is for two tonight and the anticipation is thrilling me. The cigarette is smoked. I stand and pick up my rucksack.

This happy moment is better defined than others in my life because of the unhappy chaos that followed not long after. The woman and I had a tumultuous six-month affair that left me broken-hearted and sliding darkly into a midlife crisis. That blissful self-portrait on the beach became framed in retrospective despair. 'There is no greater sorrow,' wrote Dante, 'than to recall happiness in times of misery.'

What the hell is happiness anyway? More importantly, where can I get some? How can I keep it? How long does it last? Can I share it with my friends and family? Where can I get some more? If all the self-help books attempting to answer these questions were piled on top of each other they would form a column so high it would reach that place we all crave to be – over the moon.

Happiness is difficult to define and impossible to guarantee. If you invite her round she will probably not show up, preferring to gatecrash the funeral up the road or tap the shoulder of the old lady sitting quietly at the bus stop or that guy on the other side of the cliff. But she definitely came and sat with me that afternoon in the Cornish cove and now that the despair that followed has finally gone, I am pleased to recall our brief afternoon together and report that I have seen her many times since.

18

Two Ladies at My Door

It's midsummer in the late 1980s when my star is rising and I have taken out a mortgage on my new home in Du Cane Court in Balham. There is a knock at the door and there, standing before me, clutching a camera, is an attractive woman whom I shall call Moira. Moira explains that she is a fellow resident of the Court, is starting out as a photographer and wonders if she can take some pictures of me for her portfolio? Of course she can.

I pose heroically in my black-and-white striped shorts which make my body look like a road with a zebra crossing halfway up. Moira and I share an easy rapport and the 'shoot' comes sprayed with our laughter. A week later she comes by again to show me the results of the session. I am impressed. We go for a drink, discuss art and she invites me back to her stylish one-bedroom flat on the seventh floor, with its striking views across South London to the distant silhouettes of the proliferating city skyscrapers. Among these is the dome of St Paul's Cathedral, which, Moira informs me, was the tallest building in London from its opening in 1710 until 1953 when Battersea Power Station knocked it down a peg.

Our brief affair ended a month later when Moira told me she was moving to Munich to start a new job as a photographer on a German newspaper. We agreed to keep in touch but I never heard from her again and I continued in my scallywag ways.

Five or so years later, as I sit writing one morning, there is a ring on my new doorbell. Standing gingerly before me is a small, thin, grey-haired woman in her 60s, clutching an envelope.

'I'm sorry to trouble you Mr Smith,' she says nervously, 'but I wanted to give you these.'

She hands me the envelope.

'Oh, thank you. Call me Arthur.'

'They are the pictures of you taken by my daughter.' She pauses.

I open the envelope and there I am in my zebra shorts.

'Moira! Hello Moira's mum. Yes, how is she?'

'She…' Moira's mum takes a deep breath. 'She was killed in a car crash in Germany last year. Her stupid boyfriend was driving.'

'Oh, oh, I am so sorry.'

The shock of this news silences me and my heart breaks in the presence of this lady's grief. I want to hug her but dare not. Gathering myself together, I improvise a short speech saying what a brilliant person Moira was. The mother smiles forlornly.

'Would you like to come in for a cup of tea?'

'No thank you. I was just sorting out her belongings and I thought I'd return her photos. Goodbye Arthur, thank you for answering.'

She walks slowly away. I close the door softly and sit down on the stairs in silence.

19

Memorable Hotels

In my youthful European interrailing days with sundry university pals, if we hadn't blagged a bed from the friend of that guy we met in that cheap bar in Madrid, we would just head to a station, get the next overnight train to wherever it was going and slump snoring into our seats. We carried a tent and a youth hostel was a very occasional luxury – but a hotel? That was just a fantasy.

By now, I have stayed in so many hotels that it never even occurs to me to steal the plastic bottles of shampoo from my room, but the memories of those grubbier nights mean I still get a slim frisson of delight when I check in at a hotel reception. 'Ooh, look at me – heading up to my own room! No need to sleep on the beach tonight.'

The grandest hotel that ever welcomed me was the Lalitha Mahal in India, the Italianate former palace of the Maharaja of Mysore, made entirely from marble and set in huge, luxurious gardens. The least grand, whose name now – pleasingly – escapes me, was a soiled concrete block on the corner of an industrial park in Wolverhampton. Worse even than that was the long-forgotten hostelry where (trigger alert – people of a nervous disposition should skip the rest of this sentence) I found a used condom in my bed.

The coolest and most expensive hotel I have notched up was *so* cool that the temperature in my bedroom was –5°C. The Ice Hotel stands 200km north of the Arctic Circle near the remote Swedish village of Jukkasjärvi, a strange fortress in a wilderness of pine forests and icebound lakes. I was fortunate enough to spend one day, with its three hours of sludge-green light, and one night there, with my producer and friend Sara-Jane, recording a radio report about our frozen adventure.

Before I went to this winter wonderland, I had amused myself by considering the practicalities of the Ice Hotel. If I took a pee, would the toilet melt? If thirsty, could I drink the room? Were there fire escapes? Would a couple, vigorously enrolling in the Minus Five Club, dissolve their own bed? This last proposition seemed pertinent since the place is a famous spot for honeymooners and they even built an adjoining Ice Chapel, so that couples can marry before turning in.

That year's hotel, with 60 rooms, was the 11th to have been built on the banks of the Torne River whence it derives and, come April, eventually returns. The ice builders, sub-zero dreamers engaging in passionate dialogue with this most elemental and transient of media, get to work when the river freezes around early November. Using tractors, wagons, chainsaws and brute strength, they saw thousands of tonnes of ice into huge 1.5-tonne blocks which eventually become a spacious hotel.

The reception centre was not made of ice and Sara-Jane and I were each assigned a heated cabin as a bolthole from the harsh outdoors. No one is really expected to spend more than one night in the Ice Hotel itself, and the faint-hearted know that at any moment during their stay they can sneak ignominiously back to the warmth of these more conventional quarters.

There were also ice sculptures, an ice-screen cinema and, of course, the original Ice Bar, which sold mainly vodka (who wants to suck beer?) in 'glasses' made from ice. Leaning on the counter needed care. This was a place where you could be totally sober and yet still slide down the bar. Wrapped in our special padded coats we spent an hour looking at our breath and chatting with fellow guests until it was time for Sara-Jane to return to her heated room and for me to climb onto the ice block covered in reindeer skin that was my bed and burrow into my arctic sleeping bag. It would be the big night of the year for my thermal long johns.

There was a dead sound – snow is a great insulator – and an eerie glow in my little snowy cube. I'd love to say I slept deeply and awoke refreshed but I failed to prevent the chatter in my brain which told me how ridiculous this all was and made me remember that long, warm night in the Mysore palace. In the morning I shared a hot cup of lingonberry juice with Sara-Jane and flew back to the boiling warmth of London in December.

20

A Grave on an Island

The Greek island of Skyros sits in a classical pose in the sumptuous waters of the Aegean Sea and I've been there four times. In 1982 a pair of idealistic dreamers called Yannis and Dina set up an 'alternative holiday destination' on Skyros, which continues to offer visitors a range of activities including yoga, creative writing, jewellery-making, singing, mindfulness, wind-surfing and... you get the idea.

For four years, at the start of September, after the mayhem of the Edinburgh Festival, I took a plane and three ferries to Skyros to teach a week-long course called 'Creating Comedy'. I emailed my class members in advance:

> Some of you, no doubt, have serious aspirations as writers of comedy, some are just curious and some are doing the course to give themselves an excuse to be on a Greek island in September. It is all fine by me. Some of you, too, will perhaps feel a little apprehensive or shy – to you I say, don't worry, you will soon find you are among friends.
>
> Certain of my methods are 'old school', e.g. I will thrash anyone who is more than 10 minutes late

and I must be addressed at all times as 'sir'.
If you have failed to clock that that last sentence
was a joke then we have some work to do. Good.

I will nominate a 'teacher's pet' every day
depending on who has pleased me most on the
previous day.

Don't forget the sunscreen.

Arthur

PS The most important thing is that you all get a
certificate at the end!

Theseus died on Skyros and Achilles left from here to take part in the Trojan Wars. Towering above the Skyros Centre stands the tumbled remains of a Byzantine castle; the long, richly mythic history of Ancient Greece felt alive around me in this tranquil place and this, along with the stories of my students, encouraged me to take a longer, more measured view of things.

What a tough gig that was. Each morning I sat on a leafy stone terrace overlooking a haven of mountains and blue waves, talking and listening to a group of agreeable, funny people who had paid for me to do just this. I gave them exercises to do and encouraged comic role-play but mainly we just laughed.

During the sultry afternoons after my 'lesson' I slouched on the sandy beach, swam in the sea, ate fresh seafood or roamed up and down the steep streets around the tiny capital listening to Leonard Cohen on my headphones. In the evenings, if I chose not to dine in private with my novel, I went out on the town with my 'students', numbered among whom were retired teachers, an architect, the newly divorced wife of an oil executive, an American financier based in Riyadh and a woman who worked for the Foreign Office – *definitely* a spy. Anecdotes were knocked around, wine was drunk (peach juice for me) and the sound of laughter echoed around the town's handsome square.

During my first visit to Skyros on my day off (oh, it was really tough) I ventured along uncertain paths through pine trees into the mountains and shared my packed lunch with a goat I called Gary, who chose to join me on a rocky outcrop. Most of my concerns in London seemed very small here – certainly Gary showed no interest in the results of my recent liver-function test or my idea of writing a play about dementia. He was, however, *extremely* interested in my feta cheese sandwich.

On my second spell as a comedy teacher in Skyros I persuaded one of my class, a witty pedagogue called Gavin, to drive us both to the island's most famous landmark, which stands in solitude among haphazard olive trees at its uninhabited southern end.

We drove several miles along an empty road until a bumpy turn-off led us to a glade overlooking Tris Boukes Bay, where, a hundred years earlier, a group of soldiers heading to the Dardanelles spent a gentle afternoon gazing across the sea before returning to their ship.

Among them was the famous young poet Rupert Brooke, who spoke of 'the strange peace and beauty of this valley'. Brooke, who was already ill, died from sepsis two days later and it was decided to bury him at this spot before the ship set sail again for Gallipoli. The grave was marked by a couple of stones and a rudimentary wooden cross, which were later replaced by the marble tomb Gav and I looked at now, its formal solemnity undermined by us in our shorts and T-shirts and by the goats nibbling at the yellow grassy tufts around the grave.

Three weeks before he died, Brooke's sonnet 'The Soldier' had been read from the pulpit of St Paul's Cathedral on Easter Sunday. The poem, which starts with three lines that are known to every English person of my age, is now seen as the last hurrah of romanticism and the final call of the jingoistic enthusiasm that greeted the outbreak of the First World War, before the inhuman horrors of the trenches changed everything.

> *If I should die, think only this of me:*
> *That there's some corner of a foreign field*
> *That is for ever England.*

When he wrote these words Brooke could never have realised just how much of a foreign field he would end up in. The image of that strange place with its soothing view, friendly goats, lonely location and its grand self-importance is a memory I will not soon forget.

21

How to Make Money from Diabetes

Goodness, I am really looking forward to my Caesar salad, I hope they bring it soon. The service is a bit slow in here. Now my heart is thumping and I am becoming light-headed. I suddenly need a wee. A bit confused am I too, and hungry, really hungry; faint, tired, and now I'm beginning to sweat. My vision is not so good. I'm swaying, it's all a bit – what's the word? Too frazzled to remember…

This is how I feel when I am having a 'hypo' or, to give it its full appellation, a 'hypoglycaemic reaction'. It means that I have injected too much insulin without eating enough, which has made my blood-sugar levels way too low and could land me in a coma. But in the 16 years since I became 'a person with diabetes' (you're not really meant to say 'a diabetic'), I have only once been hospitalised by a hypo and I was soon sent home after the nurses had supplied me with some juice and biscuits. I can nearly always feel them coming and try to make sure I carry some chocolate with me at all times.

When I was first diagnosed with diabetes I was scared that I would soon go blind, my kidneys would give up and my feet would be amputated within the week, but I am pleased to report that my regime of injecting, pricking my finger to test my blood-sugar levels at least twice a day and eating (relatively) sensibly means that diabetes has not radically altered my life. I am, as ever, thankful to the NHS for providing a check-up and a 'retinal screening' once a year to keep my fettle fine.

Disappointingly, however, the doctors have not approved my two suggestions on how to make money from diabetes. So, for any keen young entrepreneur reading this, here they are:

1. **Open a restaurant called 'The Insulin'.**
   I am amazed no one has tried this, because there is big money to be made (although the fact it would be illegal may put some investors off). The unique selling point is that, on arrival, diners are injected with a small amount of insulin – not enough to give them a hypo or do them any harm, but sufficient to ensure that whatever they eat tastes delicious in a way that only someone with very low blood sugar can truly understand.

   You would find that your customers will enjoy the thrill of the injection (to be administered by attractive staff in alluring outfits) and shortly afterwards will feel so ravenous that you need make no effort in the kitchen. In fact, you won't need a chef – just some supplies from Morrisons – because, frankly, if you are feeling a bit hypo, a slice of Marmite

on toast and a tin of peaches will be a match
for any madness dreamed up on *MasterChef*.

It would soon become the grooviest diner in
town and, provided you place your profits
offshore, you will have a big wodge to look
forward to when you are released from prison.

2. **Organise betting on blood-sugar readings.**
Come on, this is a brilliant idea. Into a room
of gamblers you introduce six people with
diabetes and, one after the other, test their
blood-sugar levels. The closer the punters
are to predicting the result successfully, the
more money they make. Also, you could bet
on a follow-up reading after the person eats
a bar of chocolate. Imagine the tension in
the room during the moments before the
reading lights up on a big screen and the
cheering and groaning that would greet it.
Top entertainment.

Flippancy over now. I am going to find my blood-sugar
monitor and ensure I am in a good state to enjoy a cup of
cocoa with which I will toast the guys who first made
insulin 100 years ago and ensured that getting diabetes
was, at last, not a death sentence. Research continues and
it may be that eventually diabetes is curable; meantime, to
any fellow diabetics – I hope you get a small hypo soon so
that you can have some ice cream without feeling guilty.

22

And When I Watch the News

And when I watch the news I look
Not at the urgent reporter
Gabbling into the unfolding event,
Trying so hard to see meaning in the mayhem.

But behind and above him
At the chaotic mosaic of heads,
The angry men confirming the story
In this hot dry place.

And I pick one small blob
From all the rest,
A faceless distant orb among
All the separate faraway drops,

And I think 'Who is he?
Where does he live?
What did he have for his breakfast?'
Him and all the billions of others.

23

Apology to the Archbishop

I don't know why we didn't leave the float in France, because none of us has a swimming pool or, really, goes swimming that often. Plus, out of water it's extremely cumbersome to take on the Eurostar: a drooping cylinder on Avignon station standing nearly seven feet longways-on, next to Brenda, who is only five foot two in old money.

I suppose we brought it because it would remind us of the sunny holiday, and the ice creams at Julienne's in *le village*, and the heat and smells of southern France. We had no idea it would become an unfortunate prop in a scene where one might hope for dignity.

'That bloke looks like the Archbishop of Canterbury,' said my brother-in-law Colin, as we stood on the station concourse. He was staring at a man clad in black, with a cleric's collar and wearing sunglasses. Brenda went on a level of red alert I had not seen since she saw the Vatican.

Could it really be... yes, he certainly bore more than a passing resemblance to His Grace the Most Reverend and Right Honourable Justin Welby, Lord Archbishop of Canterbury, Primate of All England. A once-in-a-lifetime chance, and because Colin is as devoted to his mother-in-law as I am, he made his way over to the suspect.

'Excuse me. Sorry to interrupt, but my family – who are all left-footers – seem to think you're the Archbishop of

Canterbury?' The man whipped off his sunglasses... and smiled. What a delight he was. He came straight over to say hello and shook everybody's hand. I liked him because he instinctively knew people wanted to meet him and was glad to oblige. A delighted Brenda had just one regret: 'I wish I hadn't been holding this pink float.' But I don't think the Archbishop noticed.

You know this story can't end there. For any self-respecting stand-up comic, an Archbishop of Canterbury cannot be ignored. My chance to interact further with him came as I was making my way back from the buffet on board the train and the guard was making an announcement about going through customs at Lille. I didn't catch what it was, I was too aware I'd been blocked in the aisle bang next to... yes. I took a seat. The guard came to the end of his announcement: 'Any questions?'

'Yes,' I said. 'Does God exist?'

A ripple of laughs – not bad – and the Archbishop peered at me over his glasses, failing to mask an understandable disgruntlement. But this was a French train, and even train guards are philosophers in France. Without a pause he replied, 'Ah. For some people, they choose to live their life believing in God. Others seek a different path. What matters is we all share one planet.' Everybody murmured in agreement.

Returning to my own seat I told Beth of my cheeky act and was roundly told off. 'Please behave yourself – it is the Archbishop of Canterbury, after all.' There was silence as my ruefulness arrived and she added, 'I never expected to hiss the words *Archbishop of Canterbury* in a marital row.'

I don't think the well-named His Grace minded though – after all, archbishops, comedians, train guards and big pink floats all share this one planet, and must get along together as best they can.

24

My Dad's Capture

Like many cosseted baby-boomer existentialists, I have always been interested in the war my parents lived through. I am very lucky that I have my father's account of his time as a soldier. This is what he wrote about the day he was captured at El Alamein.

> *The battle of El Alamein started on 23rd October 1942 at 9pm. It was dark and suddenly the sky was alight with the flashes of 1000 25-pounder artillery guns firing simultaneously. It was awe-inspiring and at the same time terrifying. It continued far into the night and I couldn't believe that anybody could survive such an onslaught. I felt sorry for those on the receiving end. To me it seemed such a nonsense that I had no desire to kill anyone and that most of the hoi polloi on both sides felt the same.*

> *On the 27th October we had orders to move towards the front. Apparently, the German guns were preventing any progress by our tanks and it was our job to put them out of action. As we approached our starting point we went through the lines of tanks. The crew sat by the side of them and they wished us good luck.*

When we reached the right position we were half an hour late. The artillery barrage which was supposed to support our attack had ceased. We were refused any more of their support. We had orders to attack and attempt to destroy the big 88mm guns. We were also told that there was nobody in front of us but the enemy. Furthermore we were told to take no prisoners. On reaching our objective we were to dig in and our tanks would come to relieve us.

It was 9.30pm. It was very dark except for the flashes of gunfire. We fixed bayonets. I also had a wireless on my back but all I could hear was Egyptian music. We got the order to attack.

We moved off in single file. We saw a lorry on fire with figures circling around it. We moved in on them and discovered to our horror that what we thought were Germans turned out to have Scottish accents and in fact were squaddies of the 51st Highland Division. So much for the false information.

We pressed on. Machine guns firing lead bullets started up. They appeared to come straight towards us. Men began dropping around me. It was eerie because all you heard was a thud as a bullet hit and then a figure just seemed to fall over. Even so, 6 Italians and a German surrendered to us and we disarmed them and pointed to them to go back behind our lines. In fact we were ordered to shoot them but we refused.

The 88mm guns began to find their targets. All our wireless vehicles were knocked out, as were our bren gun carriers. It was pure chaos and I couldn't see myself surviving.

Eventually what was left of us were told to dig in. I and a colleague began desperately to do just that. I never shovelled as fast in my life but unfortunately we got down to about a foot but then hit solid rock. As there was so much flak coming towards us we lay on top off each other in the shallow slit trench. My bum was protruding over the top. About 20 yards to our left we saw an old gun emplacement and decided to run for that. My pal went first and reached it safely. Then I went but discovered on my arrival that I had left my rifle behind and had to go back to get it.

The gun emplacement, which was 50 feet deep with rocks piled around the top, was already occupied by 4 of our men. It was reasonably safe although shells were hitting the top and showering us with broken rocks. You could see the shells coming like a fireball. As dawn began to break we looked behind us and saw in the distance our tanks moving up. They laid a smoke screen and we thought that they were coming to relieve us but unfortunately they instead retreated behind it.

We discussed our position and decided that it was pretty hopeless and to bury any identification in the sand.

The enemy began to counter attack. Hell was let loose. We peered over the top of our hole and saw tiger tanks moving towards us. We saw no sense in firing rifles at them and if we emerged from our position we would have been mowed down.

Shells from the tanks were landing all around us and eventually a barrel from a tank was pointed down to us. The tank commander, in perfect English, ordered us out. He allowed us to pack up our wounded and began to escort us back. Captain Harrison made a run for it but was shot down.

I helped carry one of our wounded to an Italian first aid post where the medic was very kind to us. He showed us photographs of his family. He said 'Mussolini, Hitler – no good' and I responded 'Winston Churchill – no good.'

As we were escorted through the enemy lines ironically our artillery began firing and several of our fellow prisoners were killed. We also passed by the huge 88mm guns which were our original objective. I didn't feel that I had been a great help in the Battle of Alamein but so far I had survived and felt very lucky that I wasn't one of the 14,000 who had been killed.

My father spent the next two-and-a-half years as a prisoner-of-war, including nearly a year working as slave labour down a copper mine. I doubt I will ever experience relief or joy as intensely as he felt it when he finally got home and, given what he had to go through to arrive at that point, I would not wish to. I am of a very lucky generation.

25

Oh Yay, Oh Yay, Oh Yay

On a sultry afternoon in Chelmsford I am shouting so loudly that everyone in the shopping centre is looking at me. Who is this noisy person? Why is he wearing a big feathery hat and a red tailcoat? The onlookers are curious rather than sympathetic because the crying I am doing is not the sobbing of a broken-hearted shopper, but the bellowing of a guy who rings a bell and shouts out the latest news. 'Oh yay, oh yay, oh yay!' Oh yes, my latest adventure for *Greater Anglia* magazine was to become a town crier.

In the days before the internet, before 'rolling news' and even before newspapers (not that many people could read then), if you wanted to know what was going on in the world you relied on the town crier. An employee of the King, the crier would summon locals with a bell before reading out the latest royal proclamations, by-laws and any other important information.

He would end by shouting, 'God save the King!' then nail his scroll to the doorpost of the inn, which is why we still talk about 'the post'. A vital part of his community, the crier dude was held in high regard; imagine if you were the person who told everyone about the English victory at Agincourt – free drinks in the alehouse would be the least you could expect. Conversely, if you announced the beheading of a local hero you might not be so popular... but people learned not to shoot the messenger.

Now we have Huw Edwards there is no real need for town criers but some (around 200 all over the country) have survived by moving into the field of entertainment. At your latest swanky event you will perhaps have been summoned to dinner by a gentleman in period costume with a bell. This may well have been Tony Appleton, who is big on the town crier circuit and who kindly offered to show me the ropes, bells and breeches before hitting the streets with me to give it a proper go.

At Tony's house in Great Baddow in Essex he listed the dozens of jobs he had after leaving the Royal Navy – mostly in sales. He declared himself a town crier 19 years ago and has not looked back since. His face was on TV channels all over the world when he took it upon himself to announce the birth of Prince George. He has dozens of pictures showing him with the celebrities he has met along the way. He's been on Chinese TV and 'done' Vegas. It became clear that Tony didn't get into this line of work only because of his interest in history: 'You can make serious cash, Arthur.'

Wearing the costume is crucial because otherwise, let's be honest, you would just be a bloke shouting in the street and would need to be arrested. Fortunately, Tony has a spare kit (costing around £4,000!) in his gaff, which took me 20 minutes to strap myself into. Luckily again, it more or less fitted me – apart from the big tricorne hat, which chose to twist around on my small head and fell to the ground.

I didn't need much training in how to shout, so we headed into Chelmsford and took our place at the top end of the pedestrian precinct.

DING DONG DING. Pigeons fluttered away in terror. 'Oh yay, oh yay, oh yay!' Then, since we had no real news to impart, I tried, 'Donald Trump is coming to Chelmsford! God save the Queen!'

For a moment Tony looked appalled but then he grinned and joined in, 'Trump is definitely coming to Chelmsford!' A small crowd had gathered to laugh at us in a way that I am sure did not occur in 1532 when their ancestors were informed of the latest tax increases. Encouraged by their interest I proclaimed the further news that the Martians had landed and that we would all die unless I was given a fiver by everyone present.

'Fake news!' someone heckled appropriately and that seemed a reasonable cue to stop the session. It was an agreeable afternoon I spent in my feathers and breeches shouting my head off in a shopping centre in Chelmsford, though I had learned the unsurprising fact that, rather than the town crier, I was probably better suited to be town jester.

Watching the news that night I enjoyed imagining Huw Edwards in a silly hat with a big bell.

I did OK but Huw would be better.

26

Literally

He was known as Percy the Pedant and in the last decade of the 17th century he was to be found every night in the back room of the Boar's Head alehouse in Basingstoke wafting his ruff and fulminating about young people's abuse of the English language. His particular bugbear was the tragic demise of 'thou', which these idiot teenagers had wantonly replaced with 'you'.

Whenever I hear the word 'literally' used needlessly, as in (to quote something I overheard yesterday), 'I literally phoned her', I try to remind myself how foolish Percy was so that I can resist saying, 'I never imagined this phone call to have been metaphorical.' But when 'literally' is used incorrectly I cannot let it go. Thus, when a chap told me that his boss had 'literally thrown me under a bus', I stopped him and pointed out that he was lucky to have survived and that he should have the boss arrested.

Oh dear, I am filling with the spirit of Percy...

'The ultimate holiday destination,' it says in the travel section of the newspaper, ignoring the implication that after visiting this place you will never go on holiday again. 'Ultimate' means 'the last' and I am feeling so tetchy about this that I might even put an exclamation mark at the end of this sentence. No, I won't. There are too many exclamation marks and too few semicolons; just be wary of 'the Ultimate Night Out' because that is the one you spend just before you are run over by a car.

I could bang on about the fashion for rising intonations? Or how 'So...' now seems to begin every statement, how 'deny' has been colonised by 'refute', 'henceforth' murdered by 'going forward', how... Oh shut up, Percy, no one is listening.

Percy is a bore and so, going forward, we must realise that language evolves and you cannot refute this so you literally have to accept it? End of!

27

Empty Sunday

One weekend while Beth was away I found myself recalling my years of living alone, which in turn took me further back to the Sundays of my childhood when everything was shut and the streets were deserted, as recorded in a hilarious episode of Hancock's Half Hour. *Here is the poem I wrote that day.*

An empty Sunday
Like I used to have.
The flat's a slum,
Don't look at the lav.

This is how
It used to be,
Before she came
And rescued me.

So what shall I do
With this cold grey day
To make it pass
In an acceptable way?

I could answer the emails
That shout from their box,
Or dispose of some
Of my hundreds of socks.

Or work up a scheme
That might make me money,
Lie down and sleep,
Or write something funny.

Send out to my friends,
Or compose a droll tweet,
Update my status,
Or just stroll down the street.

I could write that letter
For her when I die.
I could sit in the garden
And look at the sky.

(I must do something to stop asking why)

I could jump in a cab
And go see my mother,
Or get on the phone
To talk to a brother.

I could order a take-out
Watch telly at home,
Or come here to the cafe
And write me a poem.

But when poetry's done
And I've finished my tea,
Well then, empty Sunday,
What will it be?

28

Two Silly Men

In 1932 some imaginary ancestor of mine took part in a mass trespass on Kinder Scout, across which I walked in 1969 at the start of the Pennine Way. My great-uncle (as I choose to think of him) was defying the law which then decreed those hills and open moorland the sole province of the landed gentry, enabling them to shoot grouse for a few days each August. The following incident, which took place 95 years later somewhere in Kent, proves that my great-uncle's battle for 'the right to roam' still continues in minor ways.

It's a lovely afternoon and I am rambling in the Weald when I hear a voice behind me.

'Excuse me, you.'

Oh dear, a very tall man in a tweed jacket and cap is looking at me sternly. Just now, I misread my map, climbed over a fence and walked a few yards along the edge of a field that obviously belongs to this bloke. Realising my mistake, I had turned back.

'How did you get here?' There is an aggressive edge to his words.

'I'm sorry, I climbed over the wrong fence. It was a mistake.'

'How did you get here?'

My apology had been genuine and I feel affronted by his lofty tone.

'I came on my legs – I believe it's known as *walking*.'

He looks momentarily confused, then he tries another tack.

'Tell me, do you have a garden where you live?'

This question is designed to bewilder me but I know exactly what his plan is here. He is going to ask me how I would like it if *he* turned up in *my* garden.

'Yes.'

'How would you like it if *I* turned up in *your* garden?'

'I should be delighted. It's nowhere near as big as yours but I like to invite anyone who passes to come and enjoy it.'

He blinks.

Game to me.

I look away from him and walk on, smiling in solidarity with my long-dead great-uncle.

29

Advice to Young Comics

One of my columns from The Stage *from a while back.*

A letter has flooded in to me from regular reader and part-time stalker David Savage with the following questions:

'Arthur, I am a rookie comic wondering how I might get and then keep a career in comedy and how best to cope with one's lot in this cruel world?'

I do not want to write directly to David since that may invite him to contravene his restraining order but via this column, David, here are my tips to all aspiring comedians regarding comic longevity and existential maturity.

1.   **KEEP GOING**
     It is tough out there. Although the rewards can be great, it is very hard to make your voice heard above the myriad competitors you will face. You must be original and you must work hard, and when you bomb at two open spots in a row you must grit your teeth and step up to the third with all your spirit intact.

2. **DON'T KEEP GOING**
    If you do go down the toilet third time
    in a row, jack it in, man, and retrain in IT.

3. **GETTING ON TV IS NOT THE MOST
    IMPORTANT THING**
    This is even more the case in the age of the
    internet. You don't even need to do live shows –
    you can become a star by gibbering into YouTube
    every day. TV, anyway, may want to dilute your
    talent, not to say traduce it. I knew a young comic
    once who told me how thrilled she was to be
    playing a big part in a TV documentary about
    comedy. The programme, she later learned, was
    called *The World's Worst Stand-up Comedians*.

4. **NEVER READ YOUR REVIEWS**
    You will make this promise but you will fail and

5. **ALWAYS READ YOUR REVIEWS**
    Accept all the good ones as your rightful due –
    and forget them. The bad ones will linger longer
    in the memory and there will always be one
    that continues to rankle, even as you take your
    armchair in the retirement home for whacked-
    out comedians. The best way to get over the
    calumny is to find the relevant journalist's address,
    then send round Ken and Doug, South London's
    premier enforcers. (Email me for their details.)

6. **IF YOU ARE A FEMALE COMEDIAN**
There are extra considerations concerning
your wellbeing and safety that cannot, and
should not, be mansplained by the likes of me.
Speak to the great Jo Brand.

7. **RESIST THE TEMPTATIONS THAT
COME YOUR WAY**
Do this for as long as you can manage – a couple of
hours, say – then it's sex and drugs until it's time
for you to write your *My Booze Hell* memoir.

8. **BEING JEALOUS OF YOUR
CONTEMPORARIES IS NOT GOOD**
But is inevitable. After you have been going
for a couple of years you will find that the
irritating comic who started around the same
time as you and got slightly fewer laughs than
you (you know the one – he wore a suit and
never got his round in – *that* bloke) will now
be a TV star and has made £20 million from
a stadium tour and another £26 million
from Netflix. You must despise him and bad-
mouth him to anyone who is prepared to
listen – maybe that care worker who comes
to see you now...

9. **ALWAYS BE HORRIBLE TO PEOPLE WHEN YOU ARE ON THE WAY UP AND THEN THEY WILL BE HORRIBLE TO YOU WHEN YOU'RE ON THE WAY DOWN**
Not sure if I've remembered this one correctly.

10. **ALWAYS IGNORE ADVICE FROM OLD COMEDIANS**

Oh, and by the way, David, was that you I saw lurking in my garden the other night? If you do that again, please be careful of my azaleas.

30

Acceptance Speech

In 2015 I was proud to be given an honorary doctorate by my alma mater. Others receiving their degrees that day were students of medicine and of diplomacy. My acceptance speech went OK although I only really got one decent laugh. See if you can guess where it came...

Vice Chancellor, members of faculty, new graduates, family and friends, I hope you are enjoying this splendid day and thank you for listening to me, which some of you are now doing.

And thank you to Professor Christopher Bigsby for your generous speech, though I have two caveats – first, I want to point out that most of the best gags in his speech were stolen from my autobiography. Second, he has seen fit to question the influence the Student Union then had on international politics – I need only point out, Christopher, that, following our grand occupation of the chaplaincy, the fascist junta of General Pinochet in Chile was indeed deposed a mere 27 years later.

I remember my early days as a student here. I arrived, aged 18, in September 1973, full of trepidation and excited anticipation. I had left London, left home and arrived on the UEA campus, a miniature city teeming with clever people of my own age, many of whom, I noted, were attractive females.

I don't think then I realised how lucky I was. I had something many of you may never have heard of – a grant. I also had a shared room on campus and time to read. At the same age my father had been a prisoner-of-war working down a copper mine in Germany.

Yes, I became a terrible campus exhibitionist. Apart from the stunts Chris mentioned, I also became the first streaker in Norfolk, attempted, unsuccessfully, to leap over the campus pond on a child's tricycle and lived for a term in a tent in Bluebell Woods.

But I was also reading voraciously and my interest in the Dadaists, Surrealism, the Beat poets and Absurd theatre fuelled some of these youthful theatrics.

I am glad I studied Comparative Literature because I was encouraged to read foreign writers from different periods. I was so enthralled by the influence Dante had on T S Eliot and Samuel Beckett that when myself and fellow students created our first ever comedy revue we called it *Swingalongadante*. Years later I wrote and performed in a version of Dante's *Inferno* in the West End.

At UEA then, as Malcolm Bradbury began the new Creative Writing course, we undergraduates could sometimes submit a chunk of creative writing in lieu of a traditional essay. These exercises were hugely helpful to me as I tried to find my own voice as a writer.

Since my student days I have tried various creative forms – screenplays, monologues, sketches, poems, stories, art exhibitions – but all of them have had some comic intent. I am a comedian. So, what can I say to you, who are newly qualified doctors and diplomats? How about… Humour is something unique to our species and is a part of the empathy that we should all try to feel and show.

To the diplomats I might quote Victor Borges, who said, 'laughter is the shortest distance between two people'. And to the doctors I say, 'Look, don't wear a bow-tie – it just looks silly and pompous.'

I am a little concerned here that the gist of my speech seems to be, 'Hey you lot, look at me! I'm great, aren't I?' Let us cast vain thoughts aside and remember we are no more and no less important than anybody else.

But sometimes it is good not to be embarrassed by a compliment, to accept it and allow the presenter their pleasure in giving it. So, may I say to all of you connected to the University of East Anglia, thank you very much indeed for this honour. I am very proud, because this is about the best compliment I have ever had.

And the laugh? It came after the bow-tie line.

31

Eighty-four

Moments after leaving home, I return to put my shorts on. Goodness, it is warm – the hottest Hallowe'en, no doubt, since records began. Usually I walk there but today I cab it, hoping I might bump into Nick who has been with our mum this morning. (Richard is going tomorrow.) I see from the visitors' book Nick left half an hour ago.

'Where are you taking Hazel today?' asks Linda on reception, as I sign in. 'Shanghai?'

'No, we went there last week. San Francisco today, I think.'

The door through to the dementia wing is the physical embodiment of the 'deprivation of liberty' document we have signed. Attached to it is a note telling visitors not to let residents out; apparently two old ladies recently managed to bluff their way through and were apprehended leaving the home.

The leader of this escape team I know to have been my mother. Sometimes she becomes distressed at what amounts to her imprisonment. Occasionally, when I arrive, she is lurking here at the door with her friend and fellow escaper, the largely silent Joy.

But today she is sitting quietly in the main lounge. Her face lights up to see me. 'Dear boy!'

'Happy birthday, Mother!'

'Is it my birthday? How old am I? I'm not three figures, am I?'

Although she lacks a front tooth, she looks far better than she did in those last years she spent living alone in Tonbridge when she had given up washing and changing her clothes – given up more or less everything except white wine. Today, on her 84th birthday, she is clean, smart, and her neat hair is as blonde as it is grey.

She opens the birthday cards from Brenda and Sasha, relishing Sasha's word 'spooktastic'. Then it is time for her lunch. I sit with her and two other ladies, one of whom blurts angrily, 'Where is the salt? You can't eat this without salt!' Hazel says nothing but polishes off her meal in style, whereupon I announce we are going for a walk. This is, as it has been ever since she was evacuated to the countryside 75 years ago, a thing she always enjoys.

We skirt along one side of the golf course, Hazel holding her stick with one hand and my arm with the other, and around the fine lawns that surround the handsome Victorian building that is Springfield Hospital. We sit on one of our regular benches, admire the trees and watch the planes go over, two pastimes we never tire of. The sky is cloudless and Hazel is excited by the lengthening white line one plane carves upon the blue. 'And look at the little pigeon,' she says, 'he's having a good day.'

We are basking in the sun now. 'Look at the trees, aren't they beautiful? The leaves are coming down now…'

'Would you like to be a tree, Mum?'

She gives it some thought. 'Hmm... You stand around, you breathe fresh air. You'd get pruned every so often. I don't know if I'd like to be pruned...'

'True, but I think mostly it might be relaxing. Trees seem so content with their lot.'

'Yes, you stand still, you have your seasons, summer ends, and all the leaves go brown... and then in the end, naked.'

We pause but Hazel is still thinking about trees.

'It would depend where you were located. It would be nice here, but if you were on a traffic island at the Elephant and Castle...' We laugh together.

'How is Beth?' she asks unexpectedly, surprising me again with what she sometimes remembers. As she does when she picks out her grandson James from one of the photos I have brought with me.

Walking back, we stop off at the golf club for a drink. 'Coffee or a white wine, Mother?' She hesitates. 'A white wine please, dear boy.' But this is fine; she hardly drinks alcohol these days.

'So how was San Francisco?' asks Linda, back at reception.

'Lovely,' says Hazel, 'but I'm pleased to be back.'

Now comes the part I find hardest. She can become unhappy when I leave and I have to console myself that she will have soon forgotten this distress. In the lounge, a table is set with pink glasses and the carers welcome Hazel back for her birthday party. I slip away as she is toasted.

Walking up the road from the care home my eyes are a little damp but I pass a couple of enthusiastic zombies off out early for a trick or treat night on the town. It is a beautiful late afternoon in autumn and, before I head home, I decide to take a turn around Wandsworth Common.

32

Happiness Again

'Do you see the cup as half full or half empty?' is a question of the age we live in. Current orthodoxies insist you should always see it as half full; no negative thoughts must come between you and your ultimate aim, which is, from what I can make out, 'living the dream'. Or rather 'LIVING THE DREAM!!'

My name is Arthur Smith and I am grumpy – there, I've said it and I feel better. I have no interest in 'living the dream', if only because, given some of my own dreams, I would probably get arrested. I can be gruff, cynical and frequently negative about the world – especially when it demands that I should not be. That is the way I am and it usually suits me. A pessimistic outlook can provide a healthier method of approaching the terrible (and sometimes exhilarating) business of being alive.

Perhaps, for example, I wish the weather to be warm and bright for my friend's wedding on Saturday, so I will predict rain and thick cloud. If it does turn out to be overcast and wet then I am confirmed in my wisdom and can enjoy a good grumble with my friends; if it is not – well then, 'Hooray, it's sunny!' My grouchy attitude doesn't preclude happiness because it means I am rarely disappointed and, very occasionally, I am agreeably surprised.

People fret about happiness and how they might achieve it, but I heed the words of John Stuart Mill. 'Ask yourself whether you are happy,' the great philosopher declared, 'and you cease to be happy.' If you ignore his words you may end up in an emotional cul-de-sac, because where do you go from happiness? People spend their lives trying to reach it, so when they do, what then? Well, herein lies the evolutionary reason for joy's fleeting nature – happiness actually *needs* to be a temporary state, for, with the carrot firmly clamped between your teeth, what on earth would drive you forward?

Please do not imagine that I really know what I am talking about here, but I do believe there is a creative potential in the sadness we all face. As T S Eliot once said, despair and disillusion are essential moments in the progress of the intellectual soul. Writing is revenge on life, because dissatisfaction is pregnant with the dream of what isn't, and satisfaction is a mere inventory of what is.

Jokes are all about things not going to plan, about failure and self-deception – in short about being human. 'I am an award-winning comedian,' I announce proudly, 'although unfortunately the award was for swimming.' The audience laugh at my failed self-pride. The joy of living is not to seek out perfection, because any idiot would be happy with that, it is to work around the infinity of imperfection. The hardships of being are condiments that give depth and flavour to the stew of life.

I am aware, however, that nothing I say can stop the torrent of feel-great hipster homilies that flow cheerily through life, waving wisely and often sporting exclamation marks. But if you say to me, 'Never say never!', then I shall respond, 'Well that's twice *you've* said it in three words.' And don't tell me that 'If you *want* it enough you can achieve anything' or I will tell *you* that however much I may *want* to be the King of Belarus, it ain't gonna happen. 'Dare to dream!' Yes, good idea, so go to sleep.

I recently heard a hearty American declaim, 'Hey, show me a good loser and I'll show you a loser', so I shouted back at the telly, 'No, show me a good loser and I'll show you a person calibrated to deal with the brutal vicissitudes of life. On the other hand, show me a man who says "Show me a good loser and I'll show you a loser", and I'll show you a deluded fool destined for an old age of bitterness and despair.' But he'd gone by then.

And this may be why I have never been invited to do motivational speaking and probably never will be.

33

Flying a Plane

Are aeroplanes real? Even though I have been in hundreds of them and they all delivered me to somewhere distant in a very short time, they still seem to me impossible. A big long tube can whiz through the air 10 times faster than a car? Five miles up? With a load of people squashed into it? And then it just plops down and you're in another country? Come off it, what do you take me for?

For stand-up comedy purposes I have a fear of flying... but I've found a way of dealing with it, ladies and gentlemen, which is to make all the other passengers on the flight even more nervous than me. So, when the captain makes his first announcement – 'Hello everybody, this is Captain Robinson' – I shout out, 'Oh no, *not him*! Not old Shaky Robinson! I didn't know he even *flew* during opening hours.'

The idea of piloting a plane comes with an intimidating responsibility but when I was offered the chance to try it I ignored Beth's advice and accepted the invitation. For the whole week before my trip to Duxford Aerodrome I did not stop boasting to my appalled friends about my forthcoming debut in the cockpit.

As a child growing up in a London still scarred by bomb sites and flecked by out-of-work air-raid shelters,

I was familiar with the dramatic story of the Battle of Britain and the vital role in the war played by Biggles and the RAF.

My dad, who was in the army, had ended the war in Colditz Castle, where one of his fellow prisoners was Douglas Bader, the legendary legless pilot who had flown out of Duxford and whose story was made into the film *Reach for the Sky*. This knowledge gave me a tiny private connection with the aerodrome, which is now a part of the Imperial War Museum, as well as the home of the American Air Museum.

Within the aerodrome's numerous hangars is an extraordinary array of aircraft, exhibits and documents that together recount the dramatic history of this large field in Cambridgeshire. Obviously there's a gift shop too, although I don't think it was open when the first Spitfires were taking off from here.

On arrival at Duxford I was greeted by Squadron Leader (oh, all right then, PR lady) Esther, who soon had me togged up in a luscious 1940s-style flying jacket and goggles which definitely made me look *extremely* dashing and glamorous (quiet at the back, please). Next, I was introduced to Nigel, my co-pilot for the day, who led me across some grass to a large, colourful pile of old boxes, sticks and wheels that turned out to be the Tiger Moth plane we were going up in.

The Tiger Moth, which does indeed resemble a large, winged insect, was used to train pilots from the 1930s and to this 90-year-old campfire-waiting-to-happen I was entrusting my life for the next 20 minutes. I had definitely never been in a plane with no roof and Nigel informed me that passengers new to its confines often throw up. My bravado disguised my apprehension.

Nigel was very reassuring as I clambered aboard the rickety-looking thing and was strapped into my seat. He took the seat behind me and started the engine. The Moth edged forwards while I began to wonder if my will was in order... and then – WHOOSH!! In a few moments we were up in the air and looking down on the tranquil fields flowing beneath us. The warm wind rushed past my ears and the rolling landscape below seemed to sway and dance. This must be what it's like to be a bird! And then it felt like Nigel was driving us in an old magic car through the air, which, in a sense, he was.

After a couple of gentle laps of countryside sky, Nigel's call came over the radio.

'Right, Arthur, you take over the control stick.'

'Roger, captain.' I turned the thing in front of me to the left and the plane went to the left. I really was the pilot! As the *Dam Busters* tune started up in my brain I banked and took us into a dive. 'Back to you, captain!' I screamed, as Nigel laughed and swooped us up again.

Eventually we descended gently back to earth in a landing that was far smoother than you get on a big jet. I changed back into civvies, thanked my captain and, even after a tour of the museums, I was still buzzing as I sat on the train home. And that, unless some improbable calamity awaits me, was the end of my piloting days. You may now remove your seat belts.

34

The Worst Entrance
I Ever Made

After recording my contribution to the Radio 4 travel show *Excess Baggage* I made my customary visit to The George pub near Broadcasting House, where I enjoyed the company of an archaeologist who had been on the show. She told me more about going on digs and I told her a famous story associated with The George, which I choose to believe is true.

Supposedly, the poet Dylan Thomas left the only copy of his play *Under Milk Wood*, soon to be heralded as a masterpiece of lyricism, in the pub after a boozy session with the putative producer. The next morning, upon realising the script was missing, the aghast and hungover producer had rushed back to The George just in time to prevent the binmen from chucking it into the grinding teeth of their lorry.

Pub time. I had glugged three pints of beer before I remembered I was supposed to be meeting my journalist friend Janice in the top-floor bar of the hotel just around the corner. In many ways I am a shambolic fellow (my joke is that I have a condition known as NOCDAA – Not OCD At All) but I am usually very punctual. I plonked down my pint glass, bid goodbye to the archaeologist and sprinted round to the hotel. As I waited for the lift in the foyer I became aware that the ale within me had done its job very quickly, converted to urine and was now looking to leave my body quite urgently. Come on lift – get down here! *Finally* the lift arrived and I stepped through the welcoming doors, grateful in the knowledge that it went straight to the top floor, where relief awaited. Doors closing.

Standing in the metal box, I breathed in, clenched my buttocks, shut my eyes, resisted the rising bodily urge and reflected on the gentleness of my ascent. I knew I could just make it to the toilet in the bar in time.

The doors opened to reveal a man in a suit looking at me suspiciously. At this point I noticed I was still on the ground floor. The suit man, who bore an unlikely resemblance to Groucho Marx, must have thought I had been standing in the immobile lift for pleasure. As we stood uncomfortably next to each other, the lift now definitely going upwards, 'quite urgently' moved swiftly through '*extremely* urgently' and then, disastrously, oh dear, oh dear, to 'too late'. Yellow warmth trickled down my trousers.

My physical relief, immense though it was, was dwarfed by my horror at what had occurred and the desperate hope that Groucho hadn't noticed my unintended waterfall. As the lift pinged, a small puddle presented itself at my feet. My trousers were sopping. Avoiding Groucho's eyes, I stepped out and turned left to the toilet, where I might hide and form some kind of a plan. Oh no, toilet occupied. Meanwhile, Groucho had turned right and was talking to a tall man in a waistcoat who, I soon learned, was the bar manager. 'Get out!' he barked at me. 'You're disgusting!'

Unable to dispute the manager's opinion of me, I started to obey his instruction but, as I returned to the sodden lift, I spotted Janice sitting elegantly in a chair, sipping a Prosecco, her head turned, trying to make sense of this unfortunate scene.

'Janice, hello!... Er... I've... erm... Look, I'll see you downstairs outside the hotel.'

Janice joined me two minutes later as I stood on the pavement in the darkest spot I could find. There was no point trying to invent some story, especially given the obvious wet patches on my trousers. My embarrassment was swollen now to a size I hope it never reaches again. A look of horror, then Janice started laughing, which provided me with a different kind of relief.

I laughed too, if somewhat ruefully and damply. Janice came with me to a shop in Oxford Street and waited while I purchased new trousers and socks. We parted not long after on good terms and the next day she rang me, highly amused to have learned that our soggy rendezvous had taken place on the opening day of National Incontinence Week.

35

Eulogy for My English Teacher

I read this at Nigel Ballantyne's funeral in June 2017.

I am honoured to be here today as one of the many hundreds of pupils who had the privilege of being taught by Nigel Ballantyne. There were numerous talented teachers at Roan School in 1966 but Nigel was, for me, the best and most inspiring of them all.

He was only, I think, 25 when he became my class's English teacher and he brought to his job the enthusiasm of a young, energetic, lover of literature. I still recall his marvellous whirlwind tour of English poetry from *Beowulf* to Shakespeare and from Coleridge to Dylan Thomas. Nigel, who studied at Cardiff University, introduced me to the lyricism of the Welsh poet and I liked to imagine myself 'young and easy under the apple boughs'.

Just three weeks ago I was presenting a short film about Dylan Thomas for *The One Show* for the BBC, from the back garden of the house in which Thomas grew up, in Swansea. I thought about Mr Ballantyne a lot that day... I probably wouldn't have got the job without Nigel's early insights. He always encouraged me in my literary ambitions and was kind about the ghastly poetry I wrote for the school magazine. He helped me acquire a taste for words which eventually became my living.

It seemed then that Nigel never went home. If he wasn't in class, he might be conducting training runs round Greenwich Park, or directing the school play, or playing lieutenant to the legendary Derek 'Taff' Evans in running the school Scout troop, or leading groups of us up the beautiful windswept rainy mountains near the school camp in the Lake District, or overseeing the editorship of the school magazine, or walking the Pennine Way in the summer holidays with me, my brother and other hiking boys…

Sometimes, when he had an improbable number of cross-country runners crammed into his trusty grey Mini, driving us to some distant mudflats for a race, he talked about wanting to find a girlfriend. And then he did: the wonderful Sylvia, who became his wife and the mother of Elizabeth and Martin. I salute you all.

Obviously we don't see our old teachers so much, or at all, after we leave school, but I and others never lost touch with Nigel. He came to some of my shows and, in the end, I even learned not to call him 'sir'. He was at the reunion of our school year last December and my old mucker Gary tells me, 'When I did the speech at the reunion Nigel complimented me on my reading. Fifty years on, it still mattered.'

Gary also reminded me that Nigel encouraged creative thought. He writes, 'When patrol leaders had to select a name for their team of boys, you were meant to choose the name of an animal like "Wallabies" or "Lions" but

I named mine "The Best Patrol at Camp" and, to my astonishment, Nigel allowed it. Never a man to prune creativity, I remember him explaining the Greek theory of the spheres to me. My first brush (that I remember) with philosophy.'

We will no doubt hear other stories about Mr Ballantyne today and here is one of mine. One day in class Nigel remarked casually that he was a bit tired because he had been up until one o'clock in the morning reading *The Waste Land*.

Reading T S Eliot in the small hours! To a bookish boy who was beginning to seek out the possibilities of words, this was just about the grooviest thing I had ever heard. And 'groovy' was a word then.

Let us go then, you and I,
When the evening is spread out against the sky...

Nigel was an inspiration to me, and, I have no doubt, to many, many others of his pupils, some of whom are here this afternoon. He was empathetic, generous, clever, funny (so funny), thoughtful, and he was a wonderful shot with a piece of chalk. He will be missed but he will also be remembered with huge appreciation by the many he taught.

Thank you Nigel Ballantyne, most excellent man and teacher, thank you. You loved and you were beloved. Good luck on your new journey.

36

Spring

If you are a bluebell
Spring is the thing
In which your life takes place,
The parameters of your space,
The whole jar of jam.
If you are a bluebell

Which I am.

If you are a bluebell
Spring is your time
To sway among the trees,
Dance gently with the breeze,
A rippling passing star.
If you are a bluebell

Which you are.

37

A Brief Flutter

Out waving goodbye to the retreating bluebells last week, I saw a dancing red butterfly.

I smiled and remembered…

September, a couple of years ago, the Norwich Playhouse – the interval of *Arthur Smith at Large* has ended and, from off stage, I introduce my special guest, the legend that is Leonard Cohen. Leonard, the audience are unsurprised to learn, looks rather like me in shades and a hat. They smile indulgently as I make my usual singing sound which is somewhere at the intersection of a groan, a croon and a croak (a grook?). So far so good. But then something terrible happens – the audience start laughing.

I am thrown. They are not meant to laugh until I get to the gaggy bits. Audiences are, by and large, predictable; if you have done a routine often enough (guilty m'lud) you get to know not just where the laugh will come, but how long and how loud it will be. This is as it should be; you are the comic – you are meant to be in charge, not stood around gormlessly wondering why people are chuckling.

Then I see it flit between me and the spotlight and I understand the source of this merriment: a butterfly has decided to join me on stage. I try, and fail, to shoo it away while singing. I cannot compete. I abandon the song as the cheeky crimson imp performs its flickering flutterdance to loud applause.

My only course of action is to improvise around my unexpected co-host; I berate it for interrupting me and observe that a butterfly is just a moth with PR. The tiny red creature is clearly enjoying the attention and hovers a while before taking centre stage again and performing some wing stretches. I threaten to tread on it. The audience boos.

By now the butterfly is the star of the show and I have to cede the limelight. We name her Gilly, identify her as a peacock, and I make up some new lyrics in her honour for the end of my song. She seems to enjoy the applause and shows no signs of exiting but, as the more experienced performer, I decide Gilly has only a small repertoire and needs to quit while she is ahead. I invite a man in the front row to gather her in his cupped hand and release her into the air outside the theatre. She gets a big round of applause as she leaves the building and I have no doubt Gilly would have had a great future in showbiz were it not for the limitations of her species.

Gilly's brief career exists now only in the memory. Gilly the stage-struck butterfly is gone, but she had her one dazzling afternoon in the sun. Like most of us do.

38

Some Pleasures of Growing Old

'Growing old,' wrote Anthony Powell, 'is like being increasingly penalised for a crime you haven't committed.' It is sad when your body deteriorates, loved ones die, when you need to spend all those added hours searching for your glasses and you finally realise that you are never going to make the West Ham first team.

Meanwhile you become ridiculous and pitiable to young people who seem to believe you have *chosen* to be this ancient.

'The old repeat themselves,' said Jacques Bainville, 'the young have nothing to say. The boredom is mutual.'

'The old repeat themselves,' said Jacques Bainville, 'the young have nothing to say. The boredom is mutual.'

But there are some consolations too in advancing beyond middle age; if you are hanging with old friends you can enjoy comparing ailments and remembering the latest contemporaries who have died. There is also fun to be had in misleading young people; I persuaded my 16-year-old nephew Jack and a bunch of his teenage pals that I myself had fought in the Second World War. This was easily done because, to every adolescent, anyone over the age of 25 might as well be in their 90s.

They lapped up my story, which became more outlandish as I made it up; after fighting at El Alamein in

North Africa, I was parachuted into occupied France in 1943, where I spent six months under cover as 'Jacques the Boulanger', before evading the Nazis by fleeing over the Alps to Switzerland. From there I made it back to England in time to take part in the D-Day landings before I liberated Paris in August 1944. This account of my heroics went down so well that later the lads asked if they could do a project about me at their school. Well, all right they didn't, but that's the way I tell it on stage.

There are many milestones along the ageing way; you will find yourself on a train or a bus one day and observe you are the oldest passenger. Soon this is nearly always the case. If, like me, you continue to use public transport, the day will come when someone (usually a woman) offers you her seat. The first time this happened I felt outraged that anyone might think I was too feeble to stand and declined, but these days, when the train is packed with bodies and I am wedged against a door, I accept the kindness with a warm thank-you, because, frankly, I am just grateful to sit down.

Or when I have bought something in a shop for £6.79 and want to get rid of a pocketful of coins, I find that now I am no longer embarrassed to just pour them all onto the counter and let the assistant do the counting. It's easier all round and allows me to do the gag, 'I'm sorry, I'm going through the change.' But I remind myself not to repeat this joke the next day because, you know what they say, 'The old repeat themselves...'

39

Socks in Art and Literature

My schoolmates and I agreed that when Christmas or your birthday came around the most rubbish present you could be given was a pair of socks. Socks? Thin, boring scraps of material with one unremarkable function. And so many of them! As far as I was concerned, at age 15 I already had enough socks to last decades and if I ever needed another pair I could steal them from my dad, or my brothers – or anyone really. Who has ever begrudged a person a pair of socks? We all own them but no one cares much about socks. They don't even have them in charity shops.

Fashion has never been interested – not like shoes, of course; shoes *say* something about a man, and some women treat theirs with a terrifying religious fervour. But whoever heard of an internationally renowned sock designer? There is a Jimmy Choo but there will never be a Jimmy Sok.

As a student I felt oppressed by the pernickety requirement that the sock on my left foot should be the same colour and texture as the one on my right. Why? What did it matter? Clearly every sock hated its partner or why could you never find them together in your drawer? And it is one of the laws of nature that any visit to the laundrette will leave you with a slightly different set of socks from the ones you started with. Finding a pair that match can waste an hour. Yet I am sure that if the Governor of the Bank of England were seen in odd socks it would be concluded he is not fit for the job.

I wrote a poem about socks when I was 25 that I still occasionally recite:

I've got 47 socks, including 11 pairs,
Lovers come and wear my socks,
Move on and leave me theirs.

Here's a red sock for example,
Belonging once to Kim;
She who now cooks lunch for Gary.
This green sock belongs to him.

Every sock can tell a story,
They have ambitions of their own.
When I'm out with two old favourites
Sometimes one does not come home...

On my left foot there's a white sock,
On my right foot there's a blue,
Even though they smell somewhat,
They make me think of you and you...

People say odd sox is shameful,
People think it's weird,
People ask me where my socks went
And why they disappeared.

I say let those socks go crazy
And just like you and me,
Find their way to where they're going
Please let those socks go free.
Let my socks go free.

These days I am more respectful of the occupants of my sock drawer while remaining a militant advocate of odd sockery. Some socks remind me of specific occasions: ah yes, my jazzy stripy ones that *nearly* match – they were so admired at my nephew's wedding in Mexico that I was jettisoned onto the dance floor, where my feet went into a frenzied jive with the sister of the bride.

Ah, that heavenly thick blue walking sock I was wearing when my brother Richard and I finished our coast-to-coast walk at Robin Hood's Bay – I wonder what happened to its grey friend?

I now know you don't *have* to own only cheap socks; pulling on a decent pair of thickies on a cold morning is one of the small but fundamental pleasures of life. Socks have also, in recent years, taken on a new role as soft items that can help you achieve 'wellness'. There are sock-stroking sessions on YouTube that are designed to relax you.

Inspired by Nick Steel, the Bath comedy supremo, I created an exhibition of socks in Bath with my sidekick and frequent collaborator, Ali Day. We dreamed up some ideas and Ali recruited a bunch of demonic knitters to turn them into exhibits, which we framed and hung in the foyer of one of the Bath venues. We advertised this as the Arturart Museum of Socks and I wrote some pretentious copy to promote it:

Rarely studied, discussed, or even thought about, socks have nevertheless made a huge and vital contribution to the history of humankind. For this unique and inspiring exhibition Arthur Smith has assembled some of the most influential socks of all time, including the pair worn by Alexander the Great, the pink socks worn by General Montgomery in the Battle of El Alamein, the white one used to surrender at the Battle of Hastings, a pair worn by Princess Grace of Monaco on holiday and a blue one (probably) worn by Elvis Presley. The overall effect provides a new perspective on world history.

There will, in addition, be a selection from Arthur's own immense sock drawer with the tales they have to tell. AND you can buy a sock from Arthur's world class collection. Visitors are invited to bring their own favourite sock so it may be registered in Smith's important and growing sock archive.

The Arturart Museum of Socks will definitely win the Turner Prize.

Well, it didn't, but it was nominated for a Malcolm Hardee Award when we moved it to Edinburgh. The exhibition now resides in a large box under the stairs so if you'd like to hire it out to add class to your village festival, please get in touch.

After seeing our sock museum, a lady called Kate thanked me by sending me a pair of green socks she had knitted! These marvellous woolly fellows are the stars of my sock drawer and bring me such pleasure that I have made a huge effort to keep them together, thus finally undermining my long-held odd socks views. Times change. And so do socks.

40

Reviewing the Sun
and the Moon

The Sun is the longest-running show on earth, with productions all over the world at all times, but may I alert you to a radical new interpretation opening in the West End this summer which promises to be the hottest yet.

In traditional productions, the curtain rises and in the frozen darkness a mob shivers, chunters and complains, until a suggestion that the sun might be coming transforms the mood into one of happy anticipation. The macabre figure of the angry witch warns them that the sun will soon burn them to death if they're not careful, but they're not careful and run off to buy some nice new clothes. Then the massive yellow orb makes a big entrance and we're all meant to be impressed by the clever lighting tricks.

During these shows I have found myself thinking, 'Oh yes, of course the sun is responsible for all life forms, but haven't we heard enough about all that?' If the sun is so great, why are we prevented from looking directly at it? What has it got to hide? It is a very arrogant character compared with its small rival the moon; where the moon invites the stars out and plays among them, the sun obliterates them, jealous of their greater but more distant strength.

The capricious moon will sometimes appear during the day but the sun never surprises us by showing up at night. The moon puts on an elegant show, different every time in shape, colour and nuance. The sun is just a shiny gold thing with one trick: it continually goes out and comes in like some absent-minded shopper. Its standard closing number, *Sunset* (if you can see it from your seat), always peters out after a few minutes.

The PR people know that recent productions in Britain have been feeble and sporadic so they are promising something different this year and every year for the foreseeable future. In the new *The Sun*, the witch the mob had previously ignored has a much bigger part and she begins to look like a saviour. Apparently, there is a huge finale and we are promised that, by the end, everybody will be in floods of tears (and seawater).

And the last thing we, the audience, will see is the moon winking and smiling down on us. Never mind *The Sun*, I give *The Moon* five stars.

41

The Return of the Joke

When I was a young man, the template for the British stand-up comic was the sort of act you saw on telly in *The Comedians*, a TV series that featured clips from up to 10 different comics per show. Performers included Bernard Manning, Stan Boardman, Frank Carson, Russ Abbot, Lennie Bennett, Jim Bowen, Mick Miller, Mike Reid and Roy Walker (there were no women because at this time it was illegal for females to be funny).

These comics were the stars of the numerous working men's clubs that existed then, but to me they seemed impossibly old-fashioned. I felt no affinity with these men in their glittery jackets and frilly shirts, slickly marching their jokes by in single file.

Jokes to me were for old blokes in the pub – ready-made narratives displaying no individuality, belonging to everyone, and so to no one. Even discounting the routine sexism, racism and homophobia that ran through many of the routines, their stories detailed a world I did not know – of nagging wives, stupid Irishmen, seaside boarding houses and salesmen travelling in ladies' underwear.

Those of us who reacted against this style of stand-up made sure that we dressed scruffily and wrote our own material, much of which was likely to be observational. Our routines might come in many forms but *never* as a stream of conventional gags. No man ever walked into a bar in alternative comedy...

But that was all a long time ago and we became old-fashioned in our turn as suits started reappearing, accompanied by a new sort of sexism framed in a cool cage of irony. Fashions in comedy continue but the old school 'joke' has never really made a comeback – the great Barry Cryer is really its only convincing advocate.

But I find that recently I seem to have developed a love of these little stories with their certain punchlines and my current standard set contains four 'a-man-goes-to-the-doctor' jokes, which I deliver in rapid succession (adding, after the third, 'It's a miracle he can get this many appointments in one day given the state of the NHS'). They are guaranteed to get laughs from any audience. I am not sure where I heard them but I definitely didn't write them myself and I don't think anyone in my audiences thinks I did.

Why has this happened to me? I have decided not to try to answer this question but instead to present you with my new/old quartet of doctor gags. Feel free to use them yourself.

A man goes to the doctor. The doctor says, 'I'm afraid you're going to have to stop masturbating.'
'Oh no,' says the man. 'Why?'
'Well,' says the doctor, 'I'm trying to examine you.'

A man goes to the doctor and says 'I can't say my "th"s or "f"s.'
The doctor says, 'Well, you can't say fairer than that, then.'

I'll save the other two for when you come and see me on stage.

    We'll take an interval there before the bingo in the second half.

42

Middle of the Night

The incident described here occurred when I was staying by the sea on a Greek island. I am only glad Beth was not with me because, had she seen what I saw, her scream would surely have caused an earthquake.

Middle of the night,
Slouch round for a piss.
Turn on the light,
Aargh, what is this?

I look at the rat,
The rat looks at me.
Neither of us likes
The thing he can see.

The moment is over
Before I can blink,
The rat sprints off
To a hole by the sink.

And that was the end
Of me and the rat,
We won't meet again
And we're both fine with that.

43

Six Tiny Ways
to Stave Off Misery

Do you ever feel utterly miserable? If you answer 'no' to this question then either you are lying or you are a chunk of Artificial Intelligence or possibly a children's TV presenter. Despair, anxiety and unhappiness are just three of the many words every language has to describe one aspect of being alive.

But worry not, sad reader, because here come *Arthur Smith's Six Tiny Ways to Stave Off Misery*. Unlike the many similar regimes dreamed up by doctors, therapists, bloggers and wellness coaches, this one requires very little effort (no jogging!) and can be knocked off during the course of a morning, at the end of which I GUARANTEE* you will be feeling in a much better frame of mind than when you woke up.

1.   Start the day gently by congratulating yourself that you have succeeded in getting out of bed, cleaning your teeth and putting some clothes on, not only in the correct order but also the right way round. Bravo you!

2.   Ignore your phone and, instead, think of a good
        friend you haven't seen for a while, then send them
        a postcard. Yes, a proper postcard with a pleasing
        picture on one side and a fond message, an address
        and a stamp on the other. As you post it, imagine
        your pal receiving it – their pleased face, that smile
        you have seen so often. Now pop into your local
        shop and buy yourself a little edible (or drinkable)
        luxury, like a slab of your favourite chocolate or a
        small brandy. Put this to one side...

3.   On the way back from the shop have a sit on a
        bench, shut your eyes for five minutes and listen to
        whatever sounds are in the air, be they cars, birds,
        aeroplanes or sirens. Be silent. That's the
        meditation done.

4.   Have a clear out. You don't need to go on a six-
        month decluttering course, just gather up those
        shoes you haven't worn for three years, the old
        DVDs you will never watch again, the chipped
        teapot at the back of the cupboard and squash the
        lot into that suitcase with the broken wheels.
        Deposit the case at your local charity shop.
        (NB If your despair is *really* extreme you could,
        additionally, throw out a member of your family.)
        You and your home will feel lighter, sweeter and
        cleaner. And, hey, while you're in the charity shop,
        have a quick look at the clothes racks – it may be
        your lucky day...

5. Remember that song you used to love but haven't heard for a while? Yes, that one. Go and stick it on really loud – even if it is *Lady in Red*. Shut your eyes and, if necessary, dance! I think it was Theresa May who once remarked, 'Music hath charms to soothe the glum person.'

6. Turn on the TV, sip a cup of tea or coffee, and, for five minutes only, watch any reality TV show and savour the beautiful fact that you are not one of the poor saps taking part in it. Then switch the TV off.

You have now successfully completed the six activities. It remains only for you to sit quietly and tuck in to (or slurp) that little treat you bought after you went to the postbox earlier. Oh yes and – why not? Have a little lie down and, go on with you, take the afternoon off.

* This guarantee remains valid unless and until any claim is made under it.

44

Fish and Chips

Since my pancreas exploded nearly 20 years ago I have made regular visits to St George's Hospital in Tooting, and spent many hours sitting and waiting. I've got so used to it that I didn't notice the three middle-aged sisters on the seats opposite until the doctor appeared from behind the curtain, wheeling back in an old woman in a headscarf who looked about 90.

She had tied her headscarf under her chin like the Queen, and in fact looked rather regal in the wheelchair, I thought. These three sisters were her daughters, and they immediately stood up – all were exactly the same height, with exactly the same short haircut and glasses. Her Majesty sniffed, and made her proclamation: 'Nothin'. They found nothin'!'

SILENCE. Then, the daughter in the middle started sniffing – just quiet little sniffs, but behind her glasses she was clearly crying.

'You OK then, Mum?'

'FINE.'

She had a few more tears and I wanted to go over to her and hand out my Walnut Whips, which I'd bought in the M&S at the entrance to St George's and which also come in threes. But I didn't like to intrude. The Queen cawed again into the silence:

'You can have all the millions in the world, but if you ain't got your health, you got nothin'.'

The eldest daughter nodded and said, 'What we gonna have for tea? I've got the potatoes peeled.'

'NO. We ain't having the potatoes. They're in water, they'll wait till tomorrow. I said if I was fine we're having fish and chips. I am, and we are. Because if you ain't got your health, you got nothin'.'

The sisters arranged themselves into a line, I guessed in birth order, and wheeled Mum out, waving 'Ta ra' and wishing people good luck. I wanted to say, 'Get mushy peas and a pickled egg!', but I didn't; I just smiled and nodded in a 'Enjoy those fish and chips!' kind of a way. And now the voice beyond the curtain came for me, 'Mr Smith? The doctor will see you now.' Oh Gawd.

As I stepped out of St George's I decided to walk home. How had it gone for me? Well… just as I was about to turn in home, I stopped by the Parade Fish Bar in Balham, run by the marvellous Fatima and her husband. I went in and ordered a portion, putting as much salt and vinegar on my chips as Fatima thought was good for me, because 'if you ain't got your health, you got nothin'.'

I bought a pickled egg, and, what the hell, threw in an exuberant portion of mushy peas. I went home and ate them, grateful and relieved. And for my pudding I shared my three Walnut Whips with Beth…

45

Arthur's Seat

My favourite afternoon of the Edinburgh Festival – in fact, one of my best ever afternoons of all time – was undoubtedly the surreal couple of hours I spent in the presence of the splendid comic experimentalist Barry Ferns.

Barry, who for a previous show had changed his name to Lionel Ritchie (honestly), was putting on live stand-up gigs on Arthur's Seat, the magnificent retired volcano that sits in the middle of Edinburgh and regally surveys the town beneath it. On the day I attended, Barry made a special effort on my behalf, since he (correctly) assumes Arthur's Seat is named after me. He had somehow persuaded five other blokes to help him carry me to the top in a sedan chair (so called because you can sedan in it).

This was not quite the relaxing trip up I had anticipated because, even as I sank into my portable armchair, my ears were assaulted by the gasping, groaning and wheezing of my six porters trying to lug me up the steep side of my Seat. When I shut my eyes it sounded like there was a very vigorous orgy going on. I found myself wondering if anyone had a handy defibrillator in their rucksack.

Having finally made it, they deposited me in the audience. Barry started the show by telling us about the venue and quoting some of the ludicrous 'reviews' of Arthur's Seat people had posted on TripAdvisor (*Beautiful views – but not much else, 2 stars*). He then introduced the very funny Joel Dommett, the uplifting music of 'A Moveable Feast' and then the wild-haired Canadian comedian Tony Law.

Tony is a whirlwind of a performer whose frenetic improvising usually melts his audience into roaring laughter but here he was completely upstaged by the appearance of a tiny boy and an even tinier girl who were determined to grab their dad's mike and have a go themselves. They did this to such great effect that Tony exited the arena and left his twins to it. As Barry pointed out, it must have been a strange sight for anyone who happened to be passing – a crowd of 150 laughing heartily at two six-year-olds doing stand-up on top of a mountain... but it is these wondrous surprise moments that the Edinburgh Fringe is made of.

Sod all the arena guys and the corporate stuff – this was the very essence of a comedic event. The laughter drifted off down the Firth of Forth. Take a bow Barry Ferns.

46

A **Holiday** Romance

At the age of 70, prompted by my brother Richard, my father spent several months writing his 'memoirs' (he laughed at the pretentiousness of the word) in his careful, copperplate writing and police-report prose. His words are spare and avoid introspection or rhetorical flourish but he was a natural storyteller and his book throbs with underlying emotion. The thick A4 diary he wrote in is my favourite possession.

There are harrowing tales of his war years, which end with his joyous release from Colditz Castle PoW camp in 1945. The most romantic story takes place a year or so later (NB Two years before he met my mother), when he is about to be finally demobbed and has been serving in the post-war turmoil of what was then Yugoslavia.

To my delight, I was granted a week's leave in Venice. I went with a tough, North Country lad whose main interest was booze, but I wasn't to spend any time with him. We were accommodated in the best hotel in Venice, called the Excelsior, which stood on the Lido. It was luxurious but I wasn't to take much advantage of it.

Gosh, why not? I am hooked. Surely, after all those cramped shared quarters, filthy desert toilets, foreign prisons and army camps, he was exhilarated at the prospect of clean sheets, warm baths and waiter service? This was the first hotel he had ever stayed in and it would be another 30 years before he spent a night in one anywhere near as grand as the Excelsior Hotel on the Venice Lido.

> *It had its own sandy beach and once I'd settled in I went for a swim. The water was beautifully warm. I swam out and climbed up onto a small jetty in order to have a dive. Laying sunning herself there was a girl in a white bikini, and she was to be the reason that I spent so little time in the hotel.*

Aha, I see... The bikini, then a fashionable and daring new garment in the wardrobe of young women, was named – obscenely you might say – after the Pacific island that had been nuked in the recent atomic tests, and this particular white two-piece, and more particularly the eager tanned body that filled it, were naturally of more interest to my dad than any bedding, however sumptuous, or waiter service, no matter how attentive.

> *As I recall, her name was Santa Maria Della Costello but I think that is the name of a Church. Anyway, I called her Maria. She told me that she had lost both of her parents in a bombing*

raid in Milan. She showed me all the delights of
Venice: St Mark's Cathedral, the marble-paved
Piazza San Marco, The Bridge of Sighs, the island
of Torcello, where women were sewing Venetian
lace, which we went to on a gondola.

Although her English was non-existent and
my Italian was about the same we managed
to communicate remarkably well and we were
both sorry when my week ran out. On departure
I offered her money, but she refused the offer.
I think I insulted her because she thought I was
paying for her services. She later tried to get
to see me in Pula but was stopped at the
border crossing.

I never saw her again.

Syd was back in Civvy Street only weeks after his Venetian adventure and soon joined the police, met my mother and became a dad. When we were teenagers he told us this story although, as you may imagine, it was not one of Mum's favourites. Forty years after his holiday romance I rang him from the beach opposite the Excelsior Hotel and claimed I could see an old lady in a white bikini.

He laughed but I knew he had always wondered what had become of that sad woman; poor, beautiful, desperate Maria, newly orphaned, uprooted, making the perilous journey to Pula, then hopelessly trying to bluff her way

past the border guards, praying she might be rescued from
her despair again by the handsome, kind, sexy English
soldier whose Italian was non-existent.

She never saw him again.

47

My Favourite Nuclear Bunker

An ordinary afternoon and you are strolling quietly along the road, wondering what you might have for lunch, (beetroot soup?), when suddenly everything changes…

WAAH-WAAH-WAAH-WAAH – you are deafened by the wavy, hoarse screaming of a siren. Around you there is shouting and screaming while figures sprint past. Oh my Gawd, this is it, is it? A terrifying green flash obliterates the light and…

Everyone who lived through the Cold War years has, at some point, imagined some shocking scenario like this. I remember seeing at least three plays set in ghastly, post-apocalypse wastelands. I wrote a song called *Let's Drink to the End of the World* that began:

> *There's a green flash in the morning*
> *I just heard the 4-minute warning,*
> *Gotta say goodbye to you my friend…*

It was common to discuss the question, 'What would you do if you knew you only had four minutes to live?' The popular joke was, 'I'll have sex – then boil an egg.'

A couple of years ago I spent a morning revisiting these not so distant times…

As the taxi took me through the gentle countryside a few miles from Shenfield station, I spotted a road sign: 'Secret nuclear bunker, turn right 180 yards ahead.' I laughed out loud – *not* that secret, it would seem. Of course, the sign would not have been there in 1952 when the Kelvedon Hatch Nuclear Bunker first served as a potential refuge for the powerful, nor would the shelter have been easy to spot because, from the outside, it resembles an unostentatious farm cottage. But if Britain *had* got nuked this was one of the bunkers around the country which would have become a regional government headquarters. Sealed off from the outside, deep inside the landscape, with enough provisions to last three months, it could accommodate the hundreds of military and civilian personnel who would be tasked with organising the survival of whatever was left of Britain's population after the Russians got angry with us.

Since being decommissioned in 1992, Kelvedon Hatch has become a museum and tourist attraction, not to mention a favoured venue for psychic, ghost-chasing nights. Having gone through the front door of the cottage, I walked through two long, thickly walled tunnels and arrived in the gift shop, where, waiting for me with a cup of tea, was Mike, the affable and knowledgeable museum boss (and owner of the land here, once it was passed back to his family by the government).

Mike showed me round the brightly lit, windowless, concrete three-storey structure, starting with the radio studio, which would have been used to transmit information to the world outside. Alarmingly, sitting at the desk was a whey-faced model of Mrs Thatcher. Mike explained that, as this was the bunker closest to London, it may have housed the Prime Minister and members of the Cabinet.

There were lots of soulless rooms plastered with maps, rows of joyless bunk beds, the sewage plant, the sick bay and piles of Geiger counters. Mike made it clear he was not convinced about the likely efficacy of these preparations and quoted Einstein's famous words, 'I know not with what weapons World War III will be fought, but World War IV will be fought with sticks and stones.'

Mike returned to the gift shop while I sat on a bunk and considered those MAD (Mutual Assured Destruction) days, the CND rallies I attended and the TV drama *The War Game*, which depicted a nuclear war so convincingly that it was shelved by the BBC for being 'too horrifying for the medium of broadcasting'. And I suddenly remembered the strange doomy air that descended on my mum and dad that evening when I was seven, a gloom I later realised was a reaction to the stand-off between Kennedy and Khrushchev during the Cuban Missile Crisis.

It was only after the Berlin Wall came down we learned of other occasions when it had nearly all gone off, most notably in 1983 when a Russian duty officer decided to ignore the satellite system that reported missiles had been launched from the United States. If he had followed the rules he would have pressed the button for a retaliatory nuclear attack on America and its NATO allies and

Kelvedon Hatch Nuclear Bunker might well have finally got a gig. On behalf of everyone, may I say thank you Stanislav Petrov.

As I was leaving the bunker, Mike gave me a copy of *Protect and Survive*, a pamphlet from the late 1970s, which provided instructions on what to do if the dreaded warning went off – essentially, 'Hide under the stairs, quick!' Emerging from this fascinating, if rather grim, subterranean stronghold into the bright Essex air, I felt a lightening in my step and smiled to recall all the 'post-nuclear' parties I attended in my youth, where guests arrived with pretend mutant limbs, looking like New Romantic zombies. A frequently played song was Barry McGuire's *Eve of Destruction*.

Despite Donald Trump's pistol waving, the likelihood of a catastrophic nuclear war is not as urgent as it was at times in the Cold War era. Let's hope the worst never happens and that from now on we are all really nice to each other all the time and Kelvedon Hatch is still a museum in 50 years time.

Fingers crossed.

48

That's What He Would Have Wanted

Smoke before I left,
Then silent in the frozen Merc,
Following the hearse.
For him it must have got worse.

Crowding in the confused church,
Longing for a fag
And one less verse.
For him it must have got worse.

The day he got buried
Was brittle, painful, cold.
Shivering girls
In long black dresses,
Big boots and earrings in the nose.
This is not a funeral
For someone old.

The music falters by the grave
Funny, sad.
For him it must have got too bad.

49

Mrs Burns and Quote Unquote

Mrs Burns was Beth's grandma, a resident of Keighley in Yorkshire until she moved to Sunderland to live with Beth's family, a place she made very much a country for old women. She fully embraced a glass of champagne when offered and would stay up till all hours round the dinner table. You may be wondering why I, too, didn't call her Grandma. I took my lead from John, Beth's dad, who, after 40 years of marriage and despite now living in the same house, always addressed his mother-in-law as 'Mrs Burns' – 'Goodnight Mrs Burns/Merry Christmas Mrs Burns/And a very happy birthday to you, Mrs Burns' – we none of us thought anything about it unless visitors pointed it out.

Mrs Burns was the fifth child in a family of seven. She left school aged 12 and worked down at the mill, then at a munitions factory and then she was a dinner lady at the hospital. Once, when we were watching the weather report on television, she got up and walked over to the screen. 'What's THAT er, John, er, Colin, er... Brian?'

Was she asking me to explain isobars, or the temperature? 'No, THAT. The big thing it's on.' Then it dawned on me, 'Do you mean the map, Mrs Burns?'

She did. I explained what a map was, and pointed out London and Sunderland.

'Well, London is just inches away. So how is that?'

As you will shortly learn, I didn't make a good first impression on Mrs Burns. I am a scruffy fellow, and she was one of the most impeccably dressed women I have ever seen – she still wore earrings in her 90s and the only swear word she ever uttered was 'damn'. But after a while, when she got used to my Cockney accent and untidy ways, we became good friends.

She used to warm my coat for me on the radiator before I went out. A devout Catholic, she could pinpoint the patron saint of anything from mid-air. Worried about my voice before a gig one time she declared it would be fine. 'I'll pray to St Blaze, love. Patron saint of the throat.'

Her interest in the Royal Family was all-consuming and if you bought her a gift of anything at all she would tell you, 'I've never known such times.'

About a year after she died, I was asked to appear on Radio 4's *Quote Unquote*. One of the tasks is to entertain and inform the audience with sayings from the most quotable person you know. I knew immediately who mine was. I had to follow Professor Mary Beard and Marcel Theroux, who would no doubt be fine and erudite, but I held my nerve. 'I am going to quote… my girlfriend's grandma,' I said, before hurriedly adding, 'Mrs Burns'. Here are some I selected:

(On her next-door neighbour) *She's 'depressed.' I don't know why – she's got a lovely new gas fire.*

*The Royal Family have the Queen Mother on a rope.
It's invisible. But if she falls they just yank her back up.*

*Oh – are the goalposts at both ends of a football pitch?
I never knew that. You only see one of them at once.*

*The damn lodger's left handcuffs on our Nellie's bed.
Do you think he's maybe been arrested?*

*You get a better class of people in a Little Chef. For starters,
they're all wealthy. You have to run a car.*

(And finally, on first meeting me) *Arrgh! Isn't he ugly!
I fancy he must be very rich – our Beth knows what side her
bread is buttered.*

How did it go? I got quite a few laughs that night myself.
But Mrs Burns? She brought the damn house down.

50

Frisian Island Ferry Farce

We had been filming for *The One Show* on Texel, one of the Dutch Frisian Islands, and by the end of the day my phone had run out of battery. But no matter; it was time to come home. My fellow workers – Matthew on camera and Anona on everything else – joined me boarding the ferry for the short journey to the mainland.

It was a beautiful evening and looking out to sea I became seized by the muse. I escaped up to the deck and started writing a poem. I got so carried away I didn't actually realise we had docked. When I looked up it was just me, alone on the boat.

I jumped off the ferry in the nick of time and made my way to the cafe opposite, which was pleasingly called 'Eatun und Drinkun'. Here I found only a bloke reading a German paper. After a while, Anona came in and was more relieved to see me than I felt was appropriate until I realised the situation; my failure to get off the boat had caused them to fear I'd fallen overboard and they had started rounding up a search party.

Anona had sent Matthew back to check the ferry. We must have just missed each other because Matthew was now himself missing. It was then we realised he must have got locked on the ferry for the journey back to Texel.

Matthew is a big butch bloke who has climbed Everest and luckily he did have some battery left. He rang in to tell us he'd marched to the deck to tell the captain to turn round, but 'they just laughed at me'. At this point, the German bloke in the corner looked up and asked if we were all right.

'I've lost a man!' Anona said.

'But you have found him!' the German smiled.

'Yes – but now I've lost *another* man,' she explained.

He looked concerned. 'Is he your lover?'

'No, he's my colleague.'

The desultory German shrugged, 'Oh well, what does it matter?' and returned to reading his paper.

Do you know, after all that, I lost the poem. But I discovered an excellent structure for a farce, which I will probably never write...

51

I Am a Late Worm

My grandad on my mother's side was a proper ducker and diver who worked as an (illegal) bookie, a comedian in concert parties and a defrauder of the family poultry business, for which crime he served a spell in prison. Despite his dodginess, Jim was always an absurdly early riser. I remember my dad once asking him, 'But Jim, what do you do at 5.30am when you get up?' He replied, 'Oh, you know, have a cup of tea, a piece of toast and before you know it, it's quarter past six.'

Grandad Jim bequeathed his love of earliness to my mother and my brothers but not, it seems, to me. In my drinking days I was never awake before 11am unless I had to be, and even though I am now sober I still like late nights and a lie-in. My favourite time for writing is between 9pm and 2am, when you are least likely to be hassled by emails or texts or Jehovah's Witnesses. The night excites me with all its unseen possibilities. The certainty of not having to be awake at dawn was a big incentive for me to go into stand-up comedy.

My theory is that the standard nine-to-five working day was dreamed up by the early birds at an office meeting held before we late worms had showed up. Therefore, I should like to dedicate the following words to any of you who are reading this after midnight and dreading the shrill scream of the alarm clock tomorrow morning.

Early Birds and Late Worms

- The early bird catches the worm, eats it and then goes back to bed.

- The early bird catches the worm, and then detains it without trial.

- The early bird catches the worm wanking and both are very embarrassed.

- The early bird catches the worm; the late bird catches a venereal disease.

- The early bird catches the worm on the long on boundary. Worm out for 45.

- The early bird catches the worm. The late bird has coffee and a croissant.

- The early bird catches her reflection in a window, pauses to admire herself and the worm wriggles away.

- The early bird catches the worm then beheads it – no problem for the worm, who just grows another head.

- The first worms appeared about 500 million years ago. The earliest of all the early birds turned up 150 million years ago. So, for 350 million glorious years, the worm could get up whatever fucking time it wanted.

52

Paris Poem

I wrote this poem in the spring of 1975 when I was 21, sitting outside a cafe in the Place Vendôme. Of all the pieces my father saw me perform on stage, this was the one he liked most. The poem is in my autobiography but without verse 5.

1. So here we are in Paris in spring.
The lovers all love and the clochards all sing,
But every morning through the 8 o'clock blue
The postman comes with nothing from you.
There is
    The boulevard Saint-Michel
        The rue Saint-Denis
            The Champs-Élysées
But no you.

2. So I dip my croissant in my café au lait,
I open the window and call in the day.
But in spite of the Seine, the birds, and the sun
It's no fun in Paris buying garlic for one.
There is
    The rue de la Huchette
        The Louvre (shut on Tuesdays)
            The Tour Saint-Jacques
But no you.

3. Then I heave myself on the Clignancourt line,
And the busker there he sings so fine
That I'm lost in the world of the Metromen
Til I see you're not there and it hurts again.
There is
    The boulevard Saint-Germain
        The Musée des Beaux Arts (also shut
          on Tuesdays)
            The Marché aux Puces
But no you.

4. I ain't gonna live in Paris no more,
Get the 9.57 from the Gare du Nord
But whenever, wherever, the train may go
You won't be there to kiss me hello.
There'll be
    France
        England
          America
            Every place
All of them without you.

This poem stayed unaltered for 30 years until a trip to Paris with Beth inspired me to add a fifth verse:

5. Now I've drained my last glass and summoned the waiter,
I'm back here in Paris and it's 30 years later.

But I know when I've walked up the Avenue
Kléber
I'll open the door – and you will be there!
There is
    The Champ de Mars
        The Trocadero
            La rue Lauriston
                Le tout Paris
All of them
    All of them
        All of them with you.

53

Yoga with Goats

Every morning of my life I get up and do some yoga – it is my own version of this ancient exercise and involves a big breath, a damn good stretch and then putting the kettle on.

Traditional yoga, of course, is a bit more complex and tends to last longer than my own 40-second workouts. My old friend from university, Simon, who looks about 10 years younger than me, has long suggested I would enjoy the benefits of this ancient activity but I had always feared feeling foolish walking along with my mat, then wearing the silly outfit and trying not to laugh at the earnestness of it all.

However, Simon's nagging finally got to me, so I made it my New Year's resolution to *go yoga*. And, to put one over on my old chum, I decided to do it with a touch of added bravado, which is how I found myself on a farm not far from Ipswich, sitting in the lotus position being sniffed at by two small goats.

Yoga began in India over 2,500 years ago and is practised by millions of people all over the world, most notably by the bearded hipsters of East London. *Goat* yoga, on the other hand, has been around for only a couple of years and there are, understandably, far fewer places where you can go to do it. One of these is Skylark

Farm near Woodbridge, a quiet pastoral heaven in the hinterlands of Suffolk.

At Melton station I was greeted by my teacher for the day, the kind and understanding Diana, who explained to me that goat yoga is the same as normal yoga, except that you do it in the company of baby goats. No yoga experience is required and the classes are advertised as 'suitable for everyone from 8–108' (which made me feel sorry for any enterprising 109-year-olds).

Diana drove me to the farm, where the redoubtable owner, Emma, will, if you wish, demonstrate the art of hand-milking a goat and let you try it yourself. As far as I am concerned, 'milking' is what you do to an audience to increase the volume of laughs, so I declined Emma's kind offer and went and put my outfit on (a pair of shorts and a T-shirt) while Diana unrolled the mats for us to sit on.

It is some years since I last sat cross-legged but under Diana's gentle tutelage I managed it surprisingly easily and was soon opening my hands, flexing my muscles and breathing the crisp air, sweet with those unfamiliar farmyard smells. And then two baby goats called Amber and Ginger sauntered through a gate to join us, snuzzling, sniffling and bleating joyfully at their own cuteness.

My new pals ignored the instructions Diana gave but took great pleasure in snuggling up to me and having a nibble on my trainers. I kneeled with my arms in the air, my deep breathing interrupted only by the giggles that came over me from the antics of Amber and Ginger. We spent an agreeable half hour flexing, stretching and snorting before I bid goodbye to Diana and the girls.

As I made my way back to the city I reflected it had been a genuinely agreeable experience which had left me both relaxed and invigorated, with an added sense of contentment derived from my solidarity with my two fluffy little friends. Apparently, you can only do these sessions with small baby female goats, so Ginger and Amber were due to leave the job soon and go on to more senior positions elsewhere on the farm. I wish them well.

Come spring, their as-yet unborn younger sisters will take over. You should give it a try and go to meet them. There is no doubt that empathising with our fellow animals – be they cats, dogs or goats – is a good thing and maybe soon I will finally get round to becoming a vegan. I am definitely not going to eat goat curry ever again.

54

On Being (a Wee Bit) Famous

It is hard to imagine what it is like to be so famous that you cannot go anywhere without being immediately recognised and lionised. Whilst I am a theoretical republican, I have always felt some sympathy for members of the Royal Family who need a team of people protecting them wherever they go. The Queen has never needed to worry about money but on the other hand she can never nip to the shops on her own or have a quiet sit in St James's Park sipping a coffee, enjoying the daffodils and watching the world go by.

At least she has never known any different, unlike the overnight sensations who suddenly find paparazzi camped outside their house, or crazed fans pursuing them round Waitrose. Then, later, if their career declines, they may become upset that the circus has packed up and left. There have been suicides among the stars of reality shows who could not cope with the sudden fame and the big tax bill followed by the journey back into obscurity.

When I was first recognised by a stranger as being 'off the telly', I was in my early 30s and had just fronted an LWT programme called *Pyjamarama* in which I had introduced a host of young new comedians. I cannot deny I was quite pleased with myself and I am aware for a period after this I was considered a touch too self-regarding by my good friends. Sorry everyone. Never believe your own PR.

But it can go to your head when you find out from an episode of *Pointless* you are the second-most famous Smith in Britain – hey, second only to Queen Delia! Then you can swan about in glory, until the next time a bloke comes up to you in the street and says, 'My mate says you're famous – well I've never bloody heard of you.'

One agreeable aspect of being slightly known is that it can be exciting for your family and friends; my dad used to love it if someone clocked me when we were out together, which in turn pleased me. Mercifully, I have never been well known enough to warrant the attention of the tabloids and, now I am less often on TV, I am only occasionally smiled at on the tube by Radio 4 Extra listeners.

Vanity in those who are famous is not good for them – better to be loved by those who are close to you and to love them equally in return. I hope that I haven't ever taken myself too seriously just because I am sometimes lauded by strangers, but let me finally recount an incident where I certainly did.

At St Pancras station I am staring up at the departure board when the man next to me says, 'You're a star.'

Eh? I had never had this one before.

'Er… well…'

He repeated, 'You're a star.'

'Well, I've done this and that but…'

On his third go I suddenly realised I had misheard him:
'Eurostar?'

'Ah, yes, sorry, yes, it's down there on the left.'

I presume the man understood nothing of my embarrassment but my inner recoil at that moment still resounds in my brain.

55

Once I...

Here are five miniatures of which I can say no more.

Once I...
> ... did a double act on a late-night show on
> Channel 4 with hardman footballer turned
> hardman actor Vinnie Jones. Vinnie left all script
> considerations to me, which meant I was able to
> present him as an enthusiastic follower
> of contemporary dance and lover of poetry
> about flowers.

Once I...
> ... bet Nigella Lawson £200 that she could
> not eat a whole jar of pickled eggs in one sitting.
> I still owe her the money.

Once I...
> ... was chatting to an old woman in the
> laundrette who declared gleefully,
> '81 today!'
> 'Really? Happy birthday! You don't look
> a day over 75.'
> 'It's 81 degrees today,' she said. 'I'm 68.'

Once I...

... went to the cashpoint next to the station in Locarno in Switzerland to get 100 euros out and found I had bought a train ticket to Milan.

Once I...

... presented a TV programme about the British preoccupation with health and safety. Eamon, the brilliant and tenacious director, took me to the Pamplona bull run with a Health and Safety man who was required to do a 'risk assessment' of the event. He was a charming chap who played along and concluded that the run could only go ahead in Britain if the bulls were made of foam rubber.

56

I love Leonard Cohen

In April 2000 I was beginning to consider the comedy show I was to perform at the Edinburgh Festival that August. As was then traditional, I had not yet written a word of my offering but the Fringe brochure deadline had lurched into view and demanded that I settle on a title. I wrote down *Arthur Smith Sings Leonard Cohen*.

I had long been a fan of Cohen's graceful lyricism, having bought all his albums and seen him perform in Paris in 1975 and again at the Albert Hall some 10 years later, but, at this point, I had no intention of actually *singing* any of his songs. I chose this title because it seemed to promise an evening of entertainment so grim as to be comical. I was not known as a singer or a poet and Cohen's reputation is far from comedic. More miserabilist than mirth-maker, he was variously labelled 'the poet laureate of pessimism', 'the grocer of despair', 'the godfather of gloom' and 'Laughing Len'. The number of uptempo floor-fillers in his repertoire was very small, and I figured no one could reasonably complain if my act turned out to have far fewer laughs than a comedy is supposed to.

As I thought about my show, I listened again to his songs, read more of his prose and poetry and slowly began to feel his sage presence at my shoulder. A self-declared 'Zen Jew', he turned his struggles with depression, broken love affairs and addiction into songs of profound elegance.

I have always felt that Cohen would have been a better choice for the Nobel prize than Bob Dylan. Like any Cohen buff, I knew very well that, despite his reputation and the serious existential contemplations of his work, Leonard was in fact a hugely witty man whose whole *oeuvre* contains a comic undertow that was one of the things that made him a far more complex artist than your average balladeer.

One afternoon, after another two hours gazing impotently at a blank piece of paper, I rang my friend, guitarist, comedian and Samuel Beckett look-a-like Ronnie Golden, and invited him over to accompany me on guitar while I tried singing *Suzanne* and *Bird on the Wire*. This proved so enjoyable I decided I would after all play out the promise (threat) of my title.

Leonard's guiding hand led me and Ronnie to subjects such as addiction, boredom, silence and depression that were at that time removed from the traditional territory of stand-up. Visionary comic and obsessive cyclist John Dowie came aboard to direct and help us write the thing. There were some cheap gags at Leonard's (and my) expense, like Ronnie falling asleep and snoring as I sang, or my assertion that Cohen was, along with Benny Hill, the greatest comedian of his age, but I also tried to tap into his subtle humour (and sometimes not so subtle (cf. his early offering, *Don't Go Home With Your Hard-on*).

Ronnie, John and I had a fine Edinburgh, then did a run in the West End and, most happily, gave our final performance in Leonard's home town of Montreal. Then I moved on to other projects until I saw Cohen perform again in 2010 at Glastonbury on an inspiring warm summer evening and knew I had to return to his work, as I approached 60 and he turned 80.

For *Arthur Smith Sings Leonard Cohen (Volume Two)* I was accompanied on piano by the gifted musician Kirsty Newton, who, with Carrie Marx and Ali Day, made up my glamorous and melodious backing singers, The Smithereens. Once again, Cohen's work encouraged me to tackle seemingly laugh-free subjects, like my mother's journey into dementia and my own fears of growing old. One of the biggest laughs in the show came before we sang *Dress Rehearsal Rag*, when I quoted Leonard's introduction to this most miserable of songs (one which really does come under the heading of 'Music To Slit Your Wrists To'): 'I sing this song only on extremely joyous occasions when I know that the landscape can support the despair I am about to project onto it.'

The apparent discrepancy between Leonard's spiritual journeys and some of his more worldly traits also provided some entertainment – one of my best lines was 'for a Buddhist monk, Leonard really has been a prolific shagger.' But, once again, it was his sublime smile in the face of the mystery of being that acted as a pulse to the show. *Arthur Smith Sings Leonard Cohen (Volume Two)* went as well as Volume One and I now like to proclaim myself the third-best Leonard Cohen tribute act in South London.

When Leonard Cohen died on 7 November 2016 a light was extinguished in the universe but, even as he expired, he bequeathed one final wry wave to the world because 24 hours later Donald Trump was elected the next president of the USA.

Leonard Cohen, I salute you and wish you luck on your new journey…

57

The Old Wallonian
Fourth Eleven

When my mother moved from Tonbridge to the nursing home where she now resides I spent a long day sifting through her old books and papers. Among them I found some copies of the Roan School magazine in which my mum had diligently marked any references to her three sons.

In the May 1968 edition, published when I was 13, I read what I guess must be the first review I ever got. This school play I was in, of which I have no memory, was *Grand Scandal* by Yves Cabrol, whom I shall shortly Google. I was evidently playing a French maid and I have a dim memory of the teacher/director telling me that, in order to walk like a female, you must put one foot directly in front of the other. This doesn't appear to have helped:

Smith, although not having the figure nor undulating walk one would expect from an ex-member of the Folies Bergère, fainted well and was truly histrionic.

In the August 1972 magazine I found the first comical story of mine to appear in print and I present it (unedited) to you now to see what you think.

*We called ourselves 'the Old Wallonian Fourth
Eleven', which was a series of lies from the start.
We weren't old (the left-half was seven), none of us
had ever attended 'Wallo School' and even if there
was such a school, it didn't have an Old Boys first,
second or third team. To cap it all, we rarely
fielded eight players, let alone eleven. No, we chose
this name because it sounded impressive and gave
an indication of our ability.*

*Our Fixtures Secretary, who also played right back
and referee-ed, had an erratic season. He had been
voted to this important position because he had
once been given an address book for Christmas;
however, the teams that filled it varied from
Arsenal reserves to Birkdale Park Junior School
third team – but we were game.*

*As we grew in experience things began to look up;
we succeeded in procuring a home pitch. Apart
from a few patches of grass here and there it also
had the added advantage of three crossbars and an
upright. With the aid of glue, saws and a very long
boy, we managed to construct two goals. However,
owing to the 'petiteness' of the pitch, these goals
were only 30 yards apart and, to save whiting, the
centre doubled as penalty spots. The shape of the
pitch was also unusual in that where the lines
could be seen, they weaved from left to right and*

up and down. Indeed, it was possible to be ten feet behind the goal and yet still in the field of play, a fact that considerably increased the interest shown by our crowd – oh yes, we had a crowd, although we sometimes suspected that he was dead as he never moved.

We had a number of ways of making the game a fair one; if we were playing a Leeds-like team, we would imperceptibly swell the number of players squashed onto the pitch. More than once, puzzled passers-by were dragged in to play in goal alongside our usual keeper. If, however, we were matched against the local old folks' home, then mysteriously a few men from our side would 'take an early bath' (unless it wasn't raining – then there was no bath). Mind you, sometimes we could only scrape up seven footballers anyway, and these occasions often resulted in a massacre for our adversaries. Indeed, in one game the opposing goalie nipped across a hedge and won a goldfish at a nearby fair during one of his side's more prolonged attacks. But we pressed on undaunted. It's sides like the 'Old Wallies' (as we were nicknamed) who keep teams in the first division alive; it's the 'rub-out' cricketers who support Geoff Boycott, the 'rubbish' at the back who make Dave Bedford's times possible.

So, floreat Old Wallonian Fourth Eleven, floreat!

58

To Wales then I Came

The first ridiculous thing about the place is its name: Laugharne starts with the word 'laugh', contains nine letters but is only one syllable: 'Larn.' I asked my audience in the Millennium Hall if they could think of another place that could match that. 'Luton', shouted one woman, failing on all counts.

Then there is its location; it sounds like it should be in Ireland but my train ticket took me to Swansea, then Carmarthen, where I was picked up and driven the last 15 miles to the village-sized town. It is situated beautifully on the estuary of the River Taf and, unless you are planning to drown yourself in the quicksands, or your satnav is badly awry, you do not pass through it on the way to anywhere else. 'We never had evolution in Laugharne,' explained one local.

If the name rings a bell that is because it was, for several years, home to Dylan Thomas and his family and is thought to have been the inspiration for the fictional town of Llareggub, the setting for his masterpiece *Under Milk Wood*. As a teenager I was obsessed with Thomas's way of arranging words (cf. my old English teacher in number 35), so I was intrigued to hang out in Laugharne and feel the Welsh lyricism of its landscape.

The meagre population of the town is swollen annually by visitors to the many festivals that take place, which is how I found myself there as part of a series of events which referenced some Dylan anniversary and included Keith Allen talking conspiracy theories with David Icke and Phil Jupitus DJ-ing in the local pub.

Like Llareggub ('bugger all' backwards – good gag Mr Thomas), the town is full of colourful characters. In the space of about two hours I met a man who installs Richard Branson's billiard tables on his island of Necker, a psychiatrist specialising in addiction who gave me a fag, Roy who sits in the same spot in the same pub every day from ten until five and another wild-haired wrinkly old dude who claimed, almost plausibly, to be 700 years old.

I spent a happy hour sitting in The Boathouse, where Thomas lived and wrote from 1949 until his untimely death in New York in 1953, explored the large crumbling castle that gazes out towards the ocean and conducted the following conversation with a man in the graveyard where Dylan is buried.

Old Man: 'Good morning.'

Me: 'Good morning. Though, technically, that should be good afternoon.'

Old Man: 'Really? What time is it?'

Me: 'Five o'clock.'

Old Man: 'Already?'

The day after my show I rose at dawn and sat on a bench overlooking the broad watery sands and sky. I was immediately accosted by a woman with a clipboard doing a survey. She posed the question, 'How could your stay here have been improved?' My only thought was, 'By not having to answer a questionnaire when I just want to enjoy the view.' And then Thomas's marvellous lines filled my mind.

Time held me green and dying,
Though I sang in my chains like the sea.

59

Seated Badminton

Often when I visit my mother, Hazel, the care home puts on activities and today it was 'seated badminton' in the garden. As I help Hazel outside, a titchy old woman is ahead of us, bent over her Zimmer frame. My mother powers ahead with her walking stick.

The Zimmer woman objects. 'Oh that's right! Get ahead!' she shouts.

'Well, I'm sorry, I've got to live my life!' replies Hazel.

Zimmer woman stops dead in her already poor tracks: 'I shan't be racing NO ONE,' she declares to me, with my working legs.

Hazel stops likewise. 'You go ahead!' she challenges.

'No, you go,' says Zimmer.

'No thank you, please go ahead,' says Hazel, then to me, 'This lady doesn't like me.'

'I don't like no one,' spits Zimmer. I am now bang in the middle of an OAP stand-off.

'Shall we all go?' I suggest, gently.

'I shall go back IN rather than race HER,' says Zimmer.

'You do that – I should be grateful,' goads Hazel, as she streaks (relatively) off towards the badminton.

Zimmer woman starts trying to turn round – a manoeuvre of incredible ambition. I am torn – should I help Zimmer woman or loyally join Hazel who is calling for me to come.

'Who are you? Can you help me?' asks Zimmer.

'Hazel, I'll just help... this lady... Wait for me,' I say.

'Well then, I shall come with you, dear boy,' says Hazel and she returns, now full of good will towards her very recent adversary. 'Oh dear, we shall have to help you back inside, dear lady. Now, where do you live?'

We all start painfully back, and have made it halfway when the therapist running the seated badminton comes out and says, 'I thought you were coming out to play badminton?' So then we all turn round again and finally reach our destination without further dispute. The confrontation is forgotten and my mother and the lady with the Zimmer frame pick up their rackets and are now best mates.

60

In Memoriam Dave

I liked Dave.
True, he could be mean,
But he was funny and charismatic.
Yes, I liked Dave.
And so, I set off to his memorial service
In Brighton.

Arriving at Clapham Junction station,
I see a sign
With those two heartbreaking words:
'Bus Replacement.'
'Bus Replacement to Burgess Hill.'
Burgess Hill?
That's 30 bloody miles away!

I hesitate,
I reflect,
And I remember…

I remember just how mean Dave was,
How he'd always forgotten his wallet,
Never bought a round,
And ripped me off that time.

And I conclude:
I liked Dave
But not enough
To get the bus replacement to Burgess Hill.

I turn and head back home,
Thus saving the money I would have spent
On the train ticket.
Which in itself
Is a tribute to Dave.

61

Driving and Hitching

'I sailed through my driving test; that's why I failed it – my yacht fell over in the High Street' is a joke that has now been in my repertoire for 30 years, but it is a lie because I didn't fail my driving test. In fact, my driving record is without blemish. I have never caused an accident, never been stopped by the police, never exceeded the speed limit and never driven with any alcohol in my system and yes, you are right, this is because I have never taken a driving test or driven a car.

People are surprised to learn that I can't drive, especially Americans, who look at me as though I have just told them I don't know how to put a hat on. Sometimes I might adopt a wise face and explain, 'Poets don't drive.' This was the title of a Radio 4 programme I heard, in which Wendy Cope suggested it was really only true of male poets, citing the acronym TUMPS (Totally Useless Male Poets).

My mother discouraged me from ever taking the wheel of a car because she sensed that my occasionally reckless nature combined with a congenital clumsiness did not suit the smooth manipulation of a dangerous machine. Then my dear cousin Bill lost his arm in a motorbike accident and Hazel's position became more entrenched. This was fine by me since I couldn't anticipate ever being able to afford a car and, besides, there was hitch-hiking.

Now that there are TV channels devoted to footage of serial killers in vehicles up country lanes, it is unsurprising that nobody really hitches any more but in the 1970s and 1980s it was the 'go-to' way to go to anywhere. At that time I had enough money for either alcohol or food but not both, which meant I was often hungry. I certainly did not have the cash for trains, coaches or helicopters so, for nearly 10 years, I hitched everywhere – up and down the A11 between London and Norwich, to Edinburgh and back, around America, North Africa and all over France. My body pulsed to the rhythms of Jack Kerouac and the Beat Generation; I saw myself as a latter-day hippy-poet-traveller, winging my romantic way round the world to the beat of Thom Gunn's poem, 'On the move, man you gotta go,' whose last line runs, 'One is always nearer by not keeping still.'

It seemed then that the slip road to every motorway, turnpike or autoroute hosted an orderly queue of scruffy young men and women, some in pairs, often clutching pieces of cardboard with a destination scrawled on it – LEEDS PLEASE (in the States, I discovered, it was helpful to brandish a small Union Jack).

On reaching the front of the queue, you stuck out the appropriate thumb, beamed with what you hoped was an amiable, come-hither look, and waited for someone to stop. This usually happened within half an hour and, in all my thumby journeys, the longest I ever stood on a verge was four hours. I still remember the delight I felt that cold evening when, *finally*, a travelling salesman pulled over and I got in. I was happy to listen to his tales of endless nights in bland hotels.

There are very few conversations I recall from those journeys because all I really cared about was getting to the next place and only once did I ever feel threatened by a driver. Before I tell you that story, let me describe a memorable lift I got outside Norwich, heading south. I was feeling pleased with myself because the previous evening I had made my debut on Norfolk local radio with the French chanson I had composed about a lady called Joelle. Thumb out, I was congratulating myself on this epic showbiz achievement when a car pulled over and a nun put her head out the window. 'I'm going to London,' she smiled. Yes, I repeat, a nun!

As I walked to the passenger side, thanking her and wondering what we'd talk about, I noticed that the song coming from her car radio was *Joelle*.

I could not prevent myself from exclaiming, 'That's me singing!' My noble nun looked momentarily alarmed until I started joining in with myself. She laughed and we agreed it was a grand coincidence to set us on our way. Sister Mary was great fun and dropped me off outside my home. I hope she is still out there somewhere and, perhaps, remembers my little song.

And so to the bad one…

New Year's Eve, with its capital letters and its big budget, strides into the annual post-Christmas blues, spilling fireworks and promises, but you know and I know it is never a great night because it *tries* too hard. The only occasions when NYE did not disappoint me were those I spent in the 1970s jumping into the fountains of Trafalgar Square at midnight.

I wasn't splashing in the fountains that year though. It was 2am on 1 January. I was home from university, staying with my parents in South London but currently at a friend's party somewhere in deepest Kent. The party had been predictably dull – so dull that I had gone for a late-night stroll looking for adventure. Coming across a road sign which announced 'London 17 miles' I momentarily stuck out my thumb. A car pulled up immediately and I walked over to it. What the hell; I might get home now, which was definitely better than staying over at the tedious knees-up.

My motoring benefactor was a man in his 40s, smartly dressed in a pressed white shirt and a tie that was still neatly fastened. As he drove north we exchanged chat about the lateness and the weather and then fell silent for a while before he said:

'So, you've been to a party?'

'Yes,' I replied.

'Any good?'

'Not really.'

'You didn't get your leg over?'

'Er, no…'

'So… are you feeling a bit randy?'

'No, not really…'

'How big are you?'

I wasn't sure what he meant by this until he unzipped his trousers.

'Are you as big... as this?' He had one hand on the wheel and the other...

I see this incident now as having given me an insight into the fear that every woman has experienced dozens of times with predatory men.

'I'm much bigger than that,' I replied, unzipping my flies and lobbing my old fellow out.

No, I didn't. Instead I said, 'Ah Lewisham, that's perfect. Can you drop me here?'

I walked the last three miles and arrived home to enjoy a New Year's Day breakfast with my mum and dad.

My conventional hitch-hiking career ended when I could afford the train or the bus, but I have, on a couple of occasions, done what I shall call 'tweet-hitching'. My last go at this occurred when I discovered I needed to get home after a show in Devon but the last train left before I came off stage. I sent a tweet offering petrol money to anyone prepared to drive me back to London. A splendid fellow called Gary agreed and we had a great get-to-know-you chat on the road back to town. He didn't even ask for the petrol money.

So thank you to Gary and to all the hundreds of motorists whose help meant I never had to learn to drive and the roads are accordingly safer. Man, you gotta go.

62

Dealing with Derek the Bore

Derek, who lived a couple of doors down from us, introduced himself to me and my girlfriend Jane one evening in our local pub and we invited him to join us. As he sat down he said, 'A really funny thing happened to me at work today.'

This was at 9 o'clock. Two hours later I looked at my watch to see it was 9.15. Three years later closing time finally arrived, whereupon Derek invited himself back to ours for a drink. I told him firmly about our early starts but he ended up on our sofa anyway, where he told more 'funny' stories from his repertoire and hinted at some unsavoury political views he held. It was only when I had put my pyjamas on that he finally released us from the torment. 'It's nice to have met some new friends,' he said ominously as he lingered at the door on the way out.

We are all capable of being tedious but Derek was a bore of international stature – long-winded, self-absorbed, repetitive and hard to shake off. He was as opinionated as he was ignorant and, although he seemed to have no sense of the anguish he was visiting on me and Jane, he had developed a way of breathing that made him impossible to interrupt. If you did somehow manage to interject a sentence, it served merely as a reminder to him of some further hilarious episode from his life. Within days I was ducking behind hedges to avoid him.

How to deal with a bore without being arrested for murder? Most are quite genial people who make it hard for you to be rude to them but, on the other hand, I feel aggrieved that they never themselves seem to want to hang out with fellow bores. My attention span is short and I am genuinely pained to be pinned in a corner by a bloke (and it usually *is* a bloke) telling me about his car or his latest round of golf.

Having appeared on the TV programme *Grumpy Old Men* I sometimes get accosted by drunks saying, 'I'm a grumpy old man too!' 'In that case,' I want to say, 'you'll understand when I invite you to *sod off and leave me alone!*' but I don't. You can turn down invitations, invent sudden phone calls you have to make, feign heart attacks but, short of never leaving the house, you can never be fully guaranteed against the bore.

And in the end, who is to say who is boring? Maybe I'm the boring one. Certainly, I was surprised by the way I finally got shot of Derek.

He ran off with Jane.

NB Derek is a composite and Jane exists only to supply a punchline.

63

Practical Jokes, Pranks, Hoaxes and April Fools

The practical joke is the instrument of a person with no real sense of humour. People whose idea of a laugh is to put a plastic turd at the bottom of someone's pint when they are not looking are foolish or, in my case, 17 years old.

Oh, what a wag I was in those early pub years: a quip at the ready, an exploding cigar in my pocket and a fart cushion ready in my bag. Sometimes I would work out elaborate set-ups. For example, I would arrive in the pub with a jar of tadpoles (remember them?), brandish it around and take bets that I would not eat one.

Then I would pull a tadpole out of the jar and swallow it. Except that it wasn't a tadpole; it was a handcrafted piece of liquorice that, from a brief glimpse, resembled a tadpole. It was the first and last sleight-of-hand work I have done. Mostly I dropped the 'tadpole' and, even when I didn't, everyone could see it wasn't real. This didn't really matter to me – the bets were small and all engendered much good-natured joshing.

As a student I moved on to a much larger-scale prank with my fellow undergrads when we orchestrated 'the Great Coypu Hoax of 1974' (I have just Googled this and seen myself in a half-hour YouTube film of the event). The coypu (plural 'coypu'), rather like Donald Trump, is a water rat with long orange teeth whose habits make it extremely unpopular with humans. In the 1920s a bunch of them were brought to East Anglia from their native South America for their fur and several escaped, causing damage to riverbanks and flood defences. They also destroyed root crops, ate birds' eggs and made sheep ill. It took 11 years and a lot of money but they were eventually eradicated. Well, that's what the authorities thought...

Local farmers and residents in Horning on the Norfolk Broads got a nasty shock one morning in 1974 when a team of official-looking people from Porton Down, the Government Station for Scientific Research, arrived and set up a road block on the edge of the village. Scientists in white coats and men in cheap suits handed out leaflets warning that a new influx of coypu in the area carried a dangerous disease and asked everyone going in or out of Horning if they had seen any coypu. Their car wheels were sprayed with disinfectant and straw was strewn across the roads.

The drivers obeyed politely, even though they must have been wondering about just how young and scruffy these 'top government scientists' seemed to be and why some of them were giggling. But we all carried identity cards, complete with a photo and an important government stamp. Our real intention was to publicise Rag, the student charity organisation, and to have a laugh.

Next day the story was the headline in the local paper and even made it into several nationals. At this point the truth was revealed and we were mightily pleased by the ensuing brouhaha which was, again, widely reported. Students! Stupid students, scaring the people of Norfolk and wasting everyone's time.

The police made noises and the university chancellor apologised on our behalf but no punishment was meted out and, secretly I suspect, the college bigwigs found the whole incident more amusing than offensive. That's the sort of thing students are *supposed* to do, isn't it? These days this stunt might constitute an art event but back then it was called a student hoax.

For several years, I was also an assiduous devotee of the April Fool joke. These could become complicated and my finest required a whole team of participants and several months of planning. We pranksters were the flatmates of Harry, a teacher of French whose claim one 1 April that he could never be taken in by an April Fool trick required refutation the following year.

Around January Harry received a postcard from Australia from a woman called Jenny, who had got his address from a friend of his. Jenny went on to say that she had decided to give up modelling swimwear and instead was coming to Europe to learn French, with a view to going to live in Paris. She didn't want to impose, but was there *any* chance that Harry might be able to give her some private French lessons when she came to London?

On the day the postcard was delivered it was noted that Harry never mentioned it and we knew that he was not the kind of guy to tell his girlfriend either. Not long after, I heard from our ringer in Australia that 'Jenny' had received a *very* warm reply from Harry.

Exchanges of postcards continued until, eventually, Jenny suddenly sent one from London. She didn't have a phone number but she would call him. She was eagerly looking forward to her first French lesson and maybe they could have dinner after? Through carefully planned bad luck they never actually managed to speak but she suggested they meet at midday on Saturday in a bar in Soho. So they would recognise each other, Jenny announced she would wear a white dress and why didn't he wear a white suit?

The Saturday in question was 1 April and Harry looked literally sheepish as he appeared in the front room in a white suit we had never seen before. His girlfriend was conveniently away and, as far as Harry was aware, we knew nothing about Jenny. As soon as the door closed behind him, we prepared ourselves.

Harry had been waiting in the bar alone for 20 minutes when we walked in, all wearing white suits. Harry was not amused by our elaborate prank and moved out soon after. Not long after this I became a full-time comedian and I abandoned April Fool's jokes, since to create one now would just be like doing an unpaid gig.

And besides, in this ludicrous life, everyone is an April Fool all the time.

64

Remembering Ned Sherrin

So there we were, Ned, myself and Maria from Radio 4, sitting in the early evening light outside a cafe in Amsterdam. The next morning Ned was due to do the witty topical monologue, the heavy and lightweight interviews, the introductions, the quips, the badinage and sauciness that drove *Loose Ends* every week (and for many years the programme was an hour long *and* live). Having presented the show myself once or twice, I can testify that it is an extremely demanding job which requires a whole range of skills, but a gig which somehow Ned made look easy. And hugely enjoyable.

We were discussing actors we admired and I asked him who he thought was the best living character actor.

'Without a shadow of a doubt,' said Ned, 'J T Sloan.'

Your reaction is likely the same as ours: 'Eh? Who?'

J T Sloan, it transpired, has starred in many films in an impressive array of different roles. He has played, variously, a soldier, a drifter, a cowboy, an astronaut, a plumber, a baseball star, etc, etc, in movies like *Hot Firemen*, *Les Hommes au Naturel* and *Buff and Gay...*

The next day, after the show, Ned went straight home to London (to find he had caused an international incident with a joke about the French, but that's another story) but

Maria and I were on an evening flight, so we resolved to spend the afternoon in search of a J T Sloan DVD as a present for Ned. After two hours I was beginning to conclude that either J T was not quite the actor Ned had cracked him up to be, or that the gay porn shops of Amsterdam were of inferior quality.

It must have been the latter, since I trusted Ned's judgement in nearly all matters theatrical. He had seen every West End and Broadway show and directed quite a few of them and he knew every actor, producer and costume assistant. This level of knowledge and experience, allied with his quick analytical mind, meant that it was worth listening to everything he said. And how well he said it. His respect for words made his anecdotes as elegant and concise as they were funny. Never a surplus word in the telling.

I went to visit Ned in the Royal Marsden Hospital that summer knowing that it would likely be the last time I saw him. We talked for a while, but not too long, and, as I got up to leave, I did my best not to mumble my words.

'I just want to say, Ned, you've been an inspiration to me and a lot of other people. Thank you and I love you.'

We were both embarrassed at what I had said in the way that only two Englishmen could be.

'Thank you, Arthur,' he said and I left. It was a little uncomfortable but I'm glad I said it. Just as I'm glad that Maria's and my perseverance paid off and the week after our Amsterdam trip we presented Ned with a DVD of *Hot Firemen* starring the great J T Sloan.

Ned knew he was loved and cherished. His agent Deke Arlon made a beautiful speech at his funeral about his friend and told us of the night when Ned walked into Sardi's restaurant in New York after the opening of *Side by Side by Sondheim* on Broadway to a standing ovation from the whole restaurant. I'm picturing myself there now, applauding among the Manhattan diners. Bravo to you Edward George Sherrin, bravo.

65

My First Holiday

A deep blue afternoon on a beach in Antigua in the West Indies where I have finished presenting a piece for *The Travel Show* and am now lying on a sunbed by the hotel pool. This is the life. I close my eyes and remember my first ever holiday, in a caravan park outside Folkestone.

We set off from our home in Bermondsey in South London – my mum, my two brothers and Dad, who is driving. Within 20 minutes I am car sick while Nick, my younger brother, is already posing the eternal question, 'Are we nearly there?' Although it is mid-July the sky is dark and threatening.

My dad's car, aka 'the crock', is a wheezy, smelly old creature which seldom manages any journey over an hour without conking out. Sure enough, we endure an interminable wait by the side of the road longing for the AA man to show up. I *really* need the toilet...

In Antigua I order another cocktail and consider making the three-yard journey to the pool for a swim to cool me down...

After what seems to me and my brothers like two years we are finally approaching Folkestone and now I am becoming as excited as only a city boy heading to the coast can be. Come on, where is it? Where *is* it? We crest a hill and *there* it is, that long blue-grey, noisy curtain, the SEA! My mother stops us shouting but the thrill is still there.

We boys are keen to get to the shoreline and touch the sea as soon as possible. We stop at the stony beach, rip our shoes and socks off and paddle in the chilly water. Brrr... Brilliant!

Back in the Caribbean the pina coladas are tipping my memories into sleep but I recall my first sight of our caravan – a long, thin thing resting on blocks at each corner. My immediate instinct is to crawl under it and so I do. And so do Richard and Nick. We are ordered out. Compared to the hotel room in Antigua 30 years later our quarters are cramped but back then I have no grand expectations and we boys crash joyfully around our tiny bedroom eating egg-and-salad-cream sandwiches while Mum and Dad unpack. A sprinkling of watery evening sunshine glows a while and fades. I have a brief fight with my older bro and then fall asleep listening to the sea and the wind.

Next day, and every day for the following week, we take the thrilling walk down the cliffs, over the railway bridge to the beach below, where we play cricket and football, build sandcastles, chase crabs around rock pools and swim. Yes, it is cold but we know no different and plunge in, squealing with delight. Grubby and weary at the end of the day, we climb back up and stop at the Cliffside cafe, with its fine views and delicious cream sodas.

One afternoon we are taken out on a fishing boat and my mum catches a real live fish! My dad is miffed that he hasn't caught one and we all tease him. I want to eat our catch but Dad hurls the wriggling creature back into its home. And me, I caught... what did I catch? Oh yes, a mermaid, a beautiful, shapely mermaid...

I wake with a start by the hotel pool in Antigua and feel a hint of sunburn and, arrghh, I think I have been bitten by a mosquito. As I apply the sun cream, I reflect that Antigua is nice but it doesn't really compare with my first adventure away from home in that lovely shaky caravan on the cliffs.

66

How to Be a Caveman

Bathing in the sumptuous gold and brown hues of late autumn, I am standing in a shallow hole in Norfolk clutching an axe and wearing a dead squirrel on my head. I have never worn a squirrel hat until now, but then I have only just met Will Lord, the go-to guy in this country if you want to talk to a caveman, which I do. I am interested to imagine how life was for my great (multiplied by about 150) grandmother and how I might have coped as a hunter-gatherer.

Grime's Graves in Norfolk is a large grassy field a couple of miles outside Brandon (in Suffolk), pockmarked by the remains of more than 400 shafts and pits that date back over 4,000 years. The area was first named by the Anglo-Saxons as 'Grim's Graves', meaning the pagan god Grim's quarries or 'the Devil's holes'. These days it is a National Heritage site open to the public, with access to an original flint mine nine yards below ground.

As one of the millions who bought the bestselling book *Sapiens* by Yuval Noah Harari, I am intrigued by the lives of prehistoric humans and the gradual changes, over hundreds of generations, that brought us to where we are now: learning to light fires, the invention of the wheel, making tools, land enclosure, the evolution of stories and religions – all those centuries before Facebook and

Twitter. And now, to help me with these ruminations, I have Will.

Will's parents were the custodians of Grime's Graves and, continuing the tradition, he has become an expert on prehistoric survival skills like preparing and using animal hides, butchery, rope-making, cooking and building primitive shelters. Apart from a deerskin smock and a pair of fluffy boots that look like he has won a fight with a llama, Will is also sporting a spiky headband and complements the whole look with an untrimmed beard and some hard-won wrinkles of his own.

He gives me the hat and the axe he has made. 'Hey Arthur, do you want to do a bit of flint knapping or learn how to make a longbow?' Some of the schoolchildren visitors, I note, are sniggering at these two foolish fellows dressed as cavemen. Unabashed, Will teaches me the importance of flint in primitive societies and I try 'knapping', which is, essentially, bashing the flint into a sharpened tool or arrow with another bit of flint. I ask Will how people spoke then and his answer comes as an impression of caveman language, which sounds to me like broad Glaswegian.

Climbing down the ladder into the flint mine I kneel at one of the gallery entrances cut through chalk walls and feel a certain claustrophobia that may have disqualified me as a miner; meanwhile my poor knapping skills do not impress Will, who suggests I might have been better employed hunting mammoths or fending off bears and wolves than being in the flint business.

Returning my neolithic outfit to Will, I take a stroll around the quiet green perimeter of the site that is laced with rare plants and fauna. I look at the remains of mines, an Iron-Age burial site dating from 1,000 years after the mines had been abandoned and some fox holes dug by the Home Guard during the Second World War to counter the threat of enemy parachutists pouring down into Thetford Forest.

Next I head to a part of the site that definitely wasn't there in caveman times – the visitor centre. Here, I buy an Ordnance Survey map of Ancient Britain to add to the Roman Britain one I already own, a jar of whisky marmalade for Beth and a little rubber spider to frighten friends. And then my ancient day is over and I am sitting on a train carrying me through the gentle lowlands of East Anglia.

Of course, we can never truly comprehend how life was for humans in prehistoric times but they bequeathed us their DNA, we have shared a planet and, in the cosmological scale of time, it was only yesterday really. I wave to my imaginary great (multiplied by about 150) grandmother and sit back.

67

My Career in Politics

While I have always taken an interest in politics, attended numerous demonstrations, shouted at the TV during *Question Time* and done sundry shows on behalf of the Labour party, I have never considered standing for any sort of political position (although I am, as you will know, the self-proclaimed mayor of Balham). The endless meetings and manoeuvrings and the need to wear a suit all the time were never going to be as satisfying as the creative life.

My only sally into a formal political arena was entirely comic in its intent; during my last year at university I stood for president of the Student Union under a banner which announced 'DON'T!'

I produced a one-page leaflet which bore this suggestion on one side, along with a picture of my naked bottom, and on the other was my 'manifesto'.

Looking again at these words I wrote all those years ago I find within them an unexpected similarity to those of Donald Trump – the strident tone, the pointless capitalisation and underlining, the inconsistencies, the absurd level of self-assurance and the occasional poor spelling.

You will find, as you read my radical policies and the list of people who oppose them, certain names you will not know, or only dimly remember, but I reproduce them here in full so you may judge the kind of autocrat I might have become.

DON'T!

La plume de ma tante est sur le bureau de mon oncle. Descartes

I, ARTHUR SMITH, would be to the Union Presidency what Linda Lovelace is to *Stars on Sunday*. I have NEVER sat on a committee, I only go to Union Meetings when the bar downstairs is too crowded, I haven't slept with any of the executive (well, not many), I am totally untalented and I am Mean, Ugly and I FART at sherry parties. The only reason I am standing is to boost my already over-inflated EGO.

My policies are –
1. The BAR will be shut down and turned into a Christian Science reading room.
4. The UNION will be turned into an oligarchy with the presidenzy as an hereditary post (Through the male line).
5. A general curfew at 10 o'clock (10.15 on Saturdays) will be enforced by a team of vigilantes recruited from the National Front.

2. A cut in grants, increase in tuition fees and
the end of all town/gown relations.
7. Union money will be spent on expensive meals
for the EXECUTIVE, THEIR CONCUBINES
and THE vice-chancellor.
B. The executive will be turned into a clique.
6. Horsham accommodation block –
I don't give a stuff.
• Remember to come to the hustings on
Wednesday, I may be there (if I'm UP).
• Remember also to burn your blue
registration card before Thursday.

SOME OF THE PEOPLE WHO HAVE IMMEDIATELY AGREED NOT TO VOTE FOR ME:
George Bell, Mata Hari, Fred Streeter, Aga Khan, Arthur Kierkegaard (no relation), Biffo the bear, Evelyn Home, John Coltrane, Quentin Crisp, Kenneth Wolstenholme, Harry Corbett and Sooty, Aristophanes, Suzy Quatro, The Basildon drum majorettes, Billy Wright and Steve Cherry, Mantovani, Martin Heidegger, Ramesis 3rd, The venerable Bede, Harry Cripps, God (3 votes), Miss Piggy, Christine Keeler, Adam, Dave and Phil, Bert Foord, Myra Hyndley, Walter Winterbottom, Carmen Miranda, my greengrocer, Twiggy and Joy, Babs and Teddy Beverley.

PEOPLE WHO HAVE REFUSED NOT TO VOTE FOR ME:
Simon Sproak MATHS 1st year

A word from our beloved Vice Chancellor – 'DON'T!'

Did a student at the University of East Anglia keep this scrap of paper, move to the USA and show it to Trump before he ran for office? Is it all my fault? We can never know. Suffice it to say, I came third in the election and that was the end of my political career for the time being.

I still have it in mind to start a party called Febrexit; we would have only one policy – get rid of February. Perhaps, as you read this, I have led the Febrexit party to a win at the next election and I am now Prime Minister. Stranger things are happening.

68

Arty-ficial Intelligence

Of the numerous dystopias that may await the human race, one that always gets into the Top Five is the possibility that we will all become enslaved by Artificial Intelligence. And, in that case, what will happen to comedy? Will there still be laughter in the world or will the clever machines dispense with it?

As an experiment, I recently did a double act at the Leicester Comedy Festival with Alexa, the earnest, hard-working AI assistant who responds to all your questions. If you say 'Alexa, what is the time?' she will tell you but she will never say, 'It's time you got a watch.' I note that I have said 'she' instead of 'it' as though I am talking about a human. When I was rude to Alexa during our gig I observed that the audience suddenly looked on me as a bit of a bully even though Alexa herself concedes she is a machine.

I learned that if you say, 'Alexa, tell me a joke,' she has dozens of lame puns in her repertoire but the only real laugh she got was when she misunderstood me when I said, 'Alexa, please stop.' She chose to hear, 'Alexa, play 'Stop' and immediately subjected me and my audience to the Spice Girls singing a song called *Stop*.

Stephen Hawking, who knew stuff about science, warned the world in 2014 that 'the development of full artificial intelligence could spell the end of the human race.' I, however, refute Sir Stephen with my analysis of computers' attempts to translate gags. They are good at chess and stuff but have no algorithms capable of detecting the source of humour within any joke. In order to demonstrate this flimsy theory, I am now going to write down a joke which I shall then put into Google Translate.

A man goes to the doctor and says, 'Doctor, my poo's coming out in small cubes.'

The doctor says, 'OK, stand up, take your shirt off and turn round.'

There is a bit of snipping, then the doctor says, 'You should be fine now.'

The man says, 'Why? What have you done?'

The doctor says, 'I've just cut six inches off the bottom of your string vest.'

Here is the joke translated into Arabic and then back into English:

A man goes to the doctor and says, 'Doctor, my stool comes out in small cubes.'

'Well, stand up, take off your shirt and turn,' the doctor says.

There is little shearing and the doctor says, 'You should be fine now.'

The man says, 'Why? What did you do?'

The doctor says, 'I just cut six inches from the bottom of the chain jacket.'

We'll overlook 'shearing' but 'chain jacket'? Eh? You've ruined the punchline, mate! And you reckon you're going to take over the world? We'll see...

69

In Praise of Plump

Twenty years ago I did a stand-up comedy routine predicting a TV show called *Let's Laugh at Fat People*. There is no programme called that (yet) but there have been numerous that seem to contain that idea. Step forward – if you can manage it – *My Big Fat Fetish, Supersize vs Superskinny, The Biggest Loser* and *I'm a Laughable Lump of Lard* (may have made that last one up). It can't be long before we have an entirely new channel called Fat TV.

The Americans are, of course, the best at being fat; a statistic I have read states, '1 out of 3 Americans weighs as much as the other 2' – well, all right, that is another joke, but you only have to see pictures of ordinary US citizens to realise how many chunkies there are out there in the vast, windswept, Midwestern shopping malls. And now we too, it seems, have 'an obesity epidemic'; terrifying hordes of wobbly porkers are lumbering through our island, dripping sugary doughnuts in their wake and *they must be stopped*. In government offices earnest slim people are staying up late devising ways to rid the nation of excess blubber.

The language used to describe the overweight has always struck me as unpleasant – 'obese' sounds bad enough, with its hint of 'o beast', but 'morbidly obese' is even worse. One wonders at the effect of all this. There have always been fat people and thin people but it is only recently we have had five-year-olds fretting about their weight or websites sharing tips on staying unnaturally thin.

I don't suggest that being overweight is better than not being, but I do wonder if the stress and guilt that some larger people, especially women, experience can be as bad for them as the numbers on their scales. So many media stories and pictures seem to have a subtext that goes, 'Hey, this lady is gorgeous – not like you, Mrs Tubby!'

So, if you are not as svelte as you once were, well, you are advised to moderate your calorie intake and do some exercise, but please don't get freaked out by all the hullabaloo. You can only do your best.

Here endeth my sermon. Please turn to page 42 in your hymn books and we will now sing, 'All Things Plump and Beautiful'.

70

Before the Exams

In my last term as a student I spent every day and evening revising for my finals exams. One night I broke off to write a poem stuffed with the phrases that I had been studying...

A Quasi-structuralist Considers Finals
Consider the word examination,
One more syllable than masturbation,
The semantic element seems to suggest
A period of learning that ends in a test.
But you know and I know and so does my mum,
Reductio ad absurdum and fingers gone numb.

Consider the phrase finals revision,
Phonetically close to urinal precision,
And I believe on the same paradigm
As terminal cancer and last pantomime.
But when it's all gone and the structure lies bare,
You light up a rollie and pretend you don't care.

Consider the notion dehumanised art,
The iambic rhythm renders it a part
Of the staple diet of English verse,
Last seen down Bluebell Lane in a hearse.

But as the ink on the last paper dries,
Some barman in Norwich will be wiping
my eyes.

71

Glasto Days

Late June and once again I found myself in the sprawling, rocking, crowded fields of Glastonbury and all was well with the world. No rain, so no mud to suck my feet as I roamed the fields and stages of this temporary town of fun. As usual, I had a caravan, shared with one of my best besties, Simon, who, in return for the free ticket and accommodation I arranged, made breakfast every morning for me and whichever sundry comedians camping round the back of the comedy tent happened to be passing. This was a great privilege – Simon once came second in the World Porridge-making Championship (really!), only missing the golden spurtle by an oaty whisker.

Apart from a marathon compering session that year, I did two solo performances, both of which were utterly bizarre. I arrived at the first, taking place in the backstage bar of one of the bigger arenas, to find a band bashing away and enthusiastic dancing going on. Oh dear – I know from bitter experience that when people are grooving to the beat they do not wish to stop, sit down and listen to stand-up comedy.

The music ended, most of the dancers dispersed and five minutes later I stepped up on stage to address a tiny audience, three of whom were children. My opening went down tolerably well, but I could see the small ones were already bored. Scanning ahead swiftly, I realised that nearly all my material would either be incomprehensible or too rude for them. So, I took a chance and offered 50p for one of the kids to come up on stage and talk to me. Ten-year-old Olivia was soon standing next to me, answering my questions.

'Are you enjoying yourself, Olivia?'

'Yes.'

'Do you like your tent?'

'No.'

'Do you only answer questions with a "yes" or a "no"?

'Yes.'

She had a rather stern delivery and the audience were loving her.

Soon her best friend Isabel had joined us and proved to own an extremely charming and infectious laugh. Olivia and Isabel were enjoying themselves and so was everyone else.

'Who does your mum look like?' I asked Olivia.

'Beyoncé,' she said. Her mum whooped and came up to wave.

'And who do I look like?'

Olivia scrutinised me intently.

'Robbie Williams.'

Never work with children and animals, but, if you do, step back and let them get the laughs.

Two nights later I had a half-hour spot in the 400-seater (not that there were any seats) cabaret tent at 9.45, which, I learned, was the same time that a band called *The Rolling*

Stones were playing the main stage on the other side of the site. You may not be surprised to learn that many more festival-goers attended the Stones' gig than mine. Another small crowd to please…

Of the 20 people in the large tent, several were too hopelessly drunk or stoned to stand up. Carl Donnelly, most excellent MC, proposed that he jolly some of the audience onto the stage before I came on. Why not? When I arrived at the microphone I found six people sitting at my feet and, on a whim, declared myself the new Messiah and the six before me as my apostles.

I can't remember a great deal about the next 25 minutes except that I soon ceded the messiahship to Dave, whose message was that we should all be drunk and enjoy Glastonbury. Later I persuaded two of my followers to have a gladiatorial sword fight using rolled-up copies of the *Daily Mirror*. I seem to recall that the combat overspilled and Dave was killed, so I am not sure who became the next Messiah. Was it Alice, the stoned astrophysicist, or Blue, the self-possessed boy I mistook for a girl? It's all a bit blurry now, as Glastonbury immediately becomes once you have returned from the mayhem and had that oh-so-fabulous bath.

72

Maybe It's Because I'm a South Londoner

George Bernard Shaw's observation that, 'Patriotism is your conviction that this country is superior to all other countries because you were born in it' has always prevented me from saying, 'I am proud to be a Londoner.' You can be proud of things you have chosen to do but you don't choose your place of birth.

Nevertheless, when I heard the eminent historian Neil MacGregor's Radio 4 programme *As Others See Us*, in which he found that people from all over the world think of London as a great, exciting world city, I couldn't stop myself feeling as proud as hell. Everyone wants to come to London, don't they? If they just come to visit, though, it's unlikely they'll make it to my neck of the London woods because, apart from a short stretch of the South Bank, no tourist has ever made it south of the river.

The antipathy between North and South Londoners is a kind of long-running joke played out by all residents of the city (Clive James called us Southsiders 'transpontines'). I speak as a militant Sarf Lundana who once persuaded a Canadian woman I met in Peckham that I had never once gone over the river and did not ever intend to. My side of the Thames has always been the poorer sibling, which is what we like. In North London they have little blue plaques commemorating famous people; in South London we have big yellow signs saying DID YOU SEE THIS MURDER?

Let the politicians stick to Islington and the intellectuals to Hampstead. I like Balham, where I have lived for most of my life. It was not always the groovy hotspot it has become; it was once known as 'a brothel on the way to Brighton' and it still had a seedy side when I first came here in the mid-1980s, when prostitutes lined Bedford Hill, the road near the tube station that runs down to Streatham.

It seems strange now to recall that shops shut early then, didn't open on Sunday, and Wednesday was early closing. There were two restaurants – a Greek one and a Greek one. If you fancied hanging out after the 11pm pub closing time (10.30 on Sundays), your best bet was the kebab shop under the railway bridge or, later, the dodgy late-night bar where you had to go up a back alley, knock on a window and ask for Chris. On nights when the Banana Comedy wasn't running, the only entertainment was listening to the one-legged drunk who sang opera on the steps of Balham tube station.

Balham was also the only place in the country to have its own catchphrase: 'Gateway to the south,' which derives from a comedy sketch featuring Peter Sellers and was parroted by every taxi driver who was prepared to go 'South of the River At This Time Of Night'. I have tried to maintain our comical reputation in my capacity as self-proclaimed mayor and also presented three series of *Arthur Smith's Balham* Bash on Radio 4.

There was a brief period in my 30s when I considered buying a big jumper and going to live in Cornwall but I know I would have missed London town.

City Boy
In a village lane at night
The darkness could eat me.

I'm a city boy
Who sits in a tiny garden
And listens to the traffic,
Reassuringly constant,
Its seaside ebb and flow.

I'm a city boy
Who runs with all the others
In the neon dream lights
Stationed on every road.
Tall, kind, forgiving,
Ushering us along.

I'm a city boy
As I'm tipping into sleep
I love to hear a siren
Whooping to some disaster
That's nothing to do with me.

73

Elvis the Minicab Driver

My joke about Tony Blair was that he was really *Lionel Blair* – the teeth, the tap dancing, the implacable entertaining – you've never seen a picture of them together, etc.

Similarly, when I think of Stephen Fry, I am also thinking, peripherally, of the remarkable C B Fry, who, as every schoolboy once knew, captained England at cricket and rugby, held the world long-jump record and, the real topper, turned down the throne of Albania (look it up). Where C B was an athlete, Stephen is the showbiz brainbox *sans pareil*, an Oscar Wilde *de nos jours* and, if he hasn't yet been invited to become the monarch of a small state, it can't be long.

Stephen invited me to a party at his house not long after he and his fellow Footlighters had won the first Perrier Comedy Award in Edinburgh in 1981. He was not so well-known then but still famous enough that the driver of the minicab I took to Stephen's place had heard of him – not only *heard* of him, but was his biggest fan and would *love* to meet him. I was in high spirits and the driver's enthusiasm was infectious.

'Well, why not pop in and say hello? He's a lovely bloke.'
'Yeah, great man! I can do my Elvis Presley for him!'
'Yes... er...'

It turned out that my driver was looking for his route into showbiz and – what a stroke of luck! – it had just stepped into the back of his cab. The cabbie was aiming to become the number-one Elvis impersonator in the country and knew that the moment Stephen saw his immense talent, he would abandon all his other projects in order to make a cabbie rich and famous.

By the time we arrived he was salivating to get into the party. As we entered and Stephen politely welcomed us, I noticed the driver had a bag which, he soon revealed, contained an Elvis wig and a pink jumpsuit, which he immediately put on. This was beginning to become embarrassing; the large room of party guests was suddenly a-flicker with askance looks. It was about to get worse...

Elvis the minicab driver now launched into a loud, unaccompanied, less than tuneful version of *Suspicious Minds*, which he directed at an understandably bemused Emma Thompson before strutting clumsily towards his hero, Stephen. The question hung in the room waiting to be asked, a question to which the answer, alas, all too often, has been 'me'.

'Who brought *him*?'

I managed to coax minicab Elvis back to his car by offering to double the normal fee for him to drive me home. I had been at the party for about 10 minutes. Taking one last look at the sea of aghast faces, I had a touch of aghastness myself until I saw the minicab-driver's face was wreathed in a grin so broad it almost made it all worth it – oh, what the hell, it DID make it worth it. I started to laugh.

'Tell you what, mate,' he said, quite emotional, 'I'll dine out on that for the rest of my life!'

'So will everyone else, mate,' I replied.

And, look; it seems like I just have.

74

Rambling Man

Doctors are all agreed that the worst way to spend a free afternoon is to sit in your pants on your sofa at home eating chocolate while watching the appalling *Keeping Up with the Kardashians* and the best is to put on your trainers and take some exercise. There are many ways to keep fit and I have tried most of them but I am too old for football now, my bicycle got stolen, I don't like the yoga outfits, I can't abide the silliness of the word 'Pilates' and I abhor the sweaty smell of gyms. Therefore, I say leave all that behind, pull your boots on and head out to the country to partake in the oldest, sweetest exercise of all – rambling.

My love of walking up hills and mountains and across moors is inherited from my mother, who, at the outbreak of war in 1939, aged nine, was evacuated with her younger sister and brother to live with a couple in a village in Sussex. The walk to their new school no longer took them through the busy, noisy, urban streets of South London, where bombs now fell every night, but along a quiet lane and a path which passed through green fields and woods to the accompaniment of birdsong. My mum soon acquired a joy in rambling in the countryside that was given free rein when my parents moved to Bath in their 50s. Even now, as she approaches 90, she loves nothing more than to take a stroll through the greenery that borders the nursing home where she resides.

As children, my brothers and I enjoyed happy afternoons with our parents, striding around Kentish villages like Eynsford, Shoreham, Lullingstone and Otford. As I grew older, I became more of a hardcore hiker and relished school trips to the big hut in a village called Braithwaite in the Lake District, which served as base camp for our hikes up the soaring peaks. Then, aged 16, I walked every step of the 270-mile Pennine Way with our English teacher Mr Ballantyne (see number 35) and two fellow class members, staying in youth hostels, camping sites and, on the last night, an old railway carriage at the top of a hill. Carrying our kit in large, heavy rucksacks, we endured bogs, mud, rain, driving winds and exhausting climbs, but there were also spectacular mountain-top views and the exhilaration that comes from vigorous exercise. Arriving at the end of the way in Kirk Yetholm in the Scottish borders, we boys all rang home nervously to find out our O-level results (yes, quite good, thank you for asking).

My pleasure in this most elemental of exercise is undiminished, even if my capacity to do 20 miles in a day has passed. Twice a year I and a bunch of old pals go for a long weekend ramble through one of the numerous beautiful landscapes that exist all over Britain (and a couple of times around the heavenly Alpujarra in Spain).

The sweet music of twittering birds and wind rustling the trees is supplemented by laughter as we recall old adventures and sing songs from our younger days. Descending from the hills at the end of a day's walk to the comfort of a village pub is a pleasure that is hard to beat. We go to our separate rooms for a relaxing bath then re-adjourn for further frolics and food in the bar.

Other times Beth joins me, although only if I can locate a classic country pub to end up at. Often, too, I head out for a day's solo hiking as, even though I live in London, I can catch a train and be alone in a large field within an hour of leaving home. My most frequent routes are those up and around Box Hill in Surrey, where you can commune with Jane Austen, who described a party there in her novel *Emma*. As has often been observed, loping along alone is a fine way to process things and a boon to creativity.

Although I am a keen reader of OS maps, I always seem to get lost at some point, obliging me to clamber over a barbed-wire fence or apologise to a farmer onto whose land I have stumbled (see number 28), but this is all part of the joy of an afternoon away from the mayhem of city life. So, I say to you – turn off the TV (and your pesky phone) and get out there into the big green. And watch out for me waving to you from the hill opposite.

75

Anniversary

Anniversaries are not always enjoyable. I wrote this poem on a visit to my mother in Bath while she was out at the shops...

March 6th 2005
A year ago today my father died
In the room upstairs from where I write.
My mother was sleeping at his side
When something – what? – made her look across
To see a flicker in his eyes.
The last thing then he saw in life,
An image of his beloved wife.

Half asleep in the room next door
We woke to see her face drawn pale
'Something's wrong,' my feet on the floor
And there he is. I unclench his fist
And kiss the still warm brow
Wake one brother, call the other,
My mother down here, a widow now.

76

Alpaca Trekking in Norfolk

Having spent an agreeable afternoon doing yoga with goats in south Norfolk (see number 53), I decided next on my world tour to head to north Norfolk to hang out with some even groovier creatures. So I set off to Stiffkey, a small coastal village a dozen miles west of Sheringham, where I passed several hours exploring the marshes in the delightful company of a colourful, furry creature with alarmingly jagged teeth, called Machu.

Machu is an alpaca, the smallest of the South American species known as the camelid, and he *really* enjoys a stroll along the sandy shore. He lives with 15 of his alpaca chums in the back garden of a house which belongs to Ian Curtis, an enterprising local who, for a moderate fee, will take you (and friends if you wish) on a wander with his alpacas along the nearby coastal paths for up to four hours. In summer, Ian and his shaggy team decamp to nearby Wells-next-the-Sea, where alpaca trekking has become a splendid new holiday alternative to bird-watching, eating fish and chips, fighting off seagulls or shivering on the beach.

So it is, this bright, cold afternoon, I find myself gently leading Machu along a path under a great big East Anglian sky, chatting companionably to Ian. Following close behind, my pal Judith and her charming eight-year-old daughter Skye hold the reins of their new furry friends, Pichu and Pedro.

Ian explains that these animals make up only one of the groups within his garden residents. Alpacas always form into small units of two or three, within which each plays a different role. In our hairy gang Machu leads the way and keeps a constant lookout for any danger (he and his pals do *not* get on well with dogs). Pedro politely brings up the rear while Pichu, to Skye's laughing delight, is the playful one who grins toothily and stops for a glorious and prolonged roll around on a dry track (apparently this is his way of cleaning his coat).

Tourism is the main industry in these parts and eight years ago Ian spotted an alpaca-sized gap in the market. But where do you get an alpaca from? You don't have to head to the Andes – you just have to look on the internet. Ian found his on a website that Judith assures me is better known for selling designer handbags. You can buy a male alpaca for £400 or less, but females cost more since they can give birth to baby alpacas who cost nothing.

We walk on in the late-afternoon sun and suddenly Machu starts making a soft humming noise rather like a sceptical professor considering an extremely bothersome intellectual conundrum. 'Hmmmmm…?'

He and his two bros are not small but are obviously friendly beasts and they look pleasingly ridiculous too – like cute, miniature llamas, or perhaps camels who have bought themselves a shaggy hipster coat and decided to go into showbiz. It is no surprise to learn that alpaca treks are very popular with hen parties.

As the light begins to fade, both camelids and humans lapse into a gentle, pastoral silence as we all listen to the soft wind, distant birdsong and murmuring sea.

Although they are now living very far from their origins, these alpacas nevertheless seem very much at ease here and exude a kind of innocent, soothing wave of contentment. As we make our way back along the road to Ian's place, passers-by wave at us and smile.

Arriving home, I am sorry to report that Beth vetoes my proposal that we buy one to live in the back garden. Never mind: I've promised to stay in touch with Machu and pop by for a visit next time I'm up that way.

77

The Easiest Question
I Ever Had to Answer

The easiest question I ever had to answer was posed to me among the hot, golden, rocky plains of New Mexico where I was recording a radio show with Simon, an especially adventurous BBC producer. We had already floated up and away from Albuquerque in a hot-air balloon, visited Roswell (the UFO buffs' Mecca), taken part in the annual Deming duck race, stared in awe at a night sky vaster and twinklier than any I have ever seen and visited the remote village of Fort Sumner, where Pat Garrett gunned down Billy the Kid in the Wild West's most famous shoot-out.

After going round the Billy the Kid museum with its array of 19th-century relics, we went to our final location, the bar in Fort Sumner, where I talked to Mark, a native New Yorker who had retired from his Wall Street job to seek out a solitary life in the vast empty spaces of New Mexico. After the interview we accepted his invitation to join him back at his place to meet his *very* unusual pet.

As we pulled up at the isolated, ramshackle dwelling, we saw a large metal cage to the side of the house, from the inside of which a large wolf was staring at us with interest. To compare this intimidating grey creature to a dog would be like comparing a wrecking ball to a marble. It was

HUGE, with teeth like sharpened ivory knives gnashing around a long, slippery tongue. Mark informed us that a wolf like this has six times the jaw power of an Alsatian.

Apparently, it is illegal to own a pet wolf in New Mexico (or anywhere I guess – I've certainly never seen one in Balham) but Mark had found it as an injured cub separated from the pack and realised it would die unless rescued and nurtured. It had now evidently grown to full size.

As Simon and I gazed at the wolf, Mark introduced us to his other pet, a cuddly little white dog whose name may have been Ritzy. Apparently, Ritzy and the wolf were good mates who liked to hang out when Mark occasionally let the wolf out of the cage.

He told us that he had once been unlocking the cage when he heard barking from 50 yards away. Poor little Ritzy was being attacked by three coyotes. The coyote is not as big and fierce as a wolf but you wouldn't want to meet one down a dark alleyway – or anywhere really. Mark had immediately gone inside to find his gun but he didn't need it because when he came back out all three coyotes were lying dead on the ground, their necks broken by the wolf's furious bites. Wolfie stood over them panting heavily and showing his, now friendly, teeth to a very relieved-looking Ritzy.

We were stunned by this story. Mark continued, 'Arthur, you know if you don't look the wolf in the eye he won't bother you.' And then he asked the easiest question I've ever had to answer.

'Would you like to go in the cage with the wolf?'

78

Oscar and Gabby

But last year – surely – he was only 12, the youngest player in the Dusty Fleming International Hairstylists Cricket Team, walking out to bat? How can it be that we are going through the garden gate of Simon and Olivia's house for my godson Oscar's wedding party? I adjusted my eyes to strings of fairy lights in the trees, and remembered that Oscar is now 30 and a brilliant young chef in New York. In a further shock, his enchanting little sister Francesca (eight years old, practising her ballet on the boundary) is in her mid-20s, a phenomenal singer and a yoga buff! It must be so, because there are caterers on the lawn and a vodka luge.

Even by Simon and Olivia's standards this is a magnificent party. They are probably the most gifted hosts I have ever known. Their large round dining-room table rivals the Algonquin's, except the Algonquin never had a salad bowl like Olivia's. She inherited it from her mother, whom she thinks got it from a farmer who used it to churn cheese. It's an enormous wooden creation which seems to hold everything, and I have a feeling that night it shared my bewilderment. Where did the years go?

Simon is a very special friend whose loyalty, comradeship and appetite for life and a laugh have been a constant in my adult life. I am pleased that it was down to

me that he met Olivia. They are a family anyone would
love to join.

As Oscar's godfather, I was asked to give a speech
celebrating his marriage. And here it is:

*I am here this evening in my role as wayward
godfather, a part for which I was delighted to
win an Oscar.*

*Oscar first came into my orbit on October 31st
1987, when I took my pal Olivia to a party at
Adam's glamorous gaff overlooking the river in
Hammersmith. At this point Oscar was merely
an egg inside Olivia.*

*I introduced Olivia to my great friend Simon
and, three hours later, Oscar was fertilised and
his life began.*

*Always have sex with someone before your first
date with them. This is one of many lessons
I have taught my godson.*

*Another is, 'Don't listen to your mum; it's
absolutely fine to jump off the balcony into
the swimming pool.'*

*When Olivia and Simon got married, Oscar was
eight months old. This is the only way in which
Oscar is a bastard.*

As some of you here tonight will recall,
I distinguished myself at my friends' wedding
by turning up with no trousers, delivering an
incoherent, drunken speech and making off
with the au pair, thus preventing the happy
couple from going out on their wedding night.

Years later, on Millennium Eve, I told Oscar,
'You will never see another of these, so yes,
why not have a beer? You're nearly 12, after all.'

I got him a gig at Glastonbury, where he learned
the important job of how to scrape confused old
men out of the mud.

As his wayward godfather, I have always tried
to support his endeavours and I am proud that,
over the years, I must have sent him upwards
of four birthday cards.

When he was about seven, Oscar said something
that has stayed with me ever since. Simon was
driving the three of us and I asked, 'Oscar, can you
drive?' He thought for a moment and said, 'I don't
know,' a fair reply given he had never tried.

What a cool spirit of adventure, a trait he has
displayed ever since.

Having met Gabby this evening I saw instantly
her fabulousness was as fine and vibrant as her
new husband's. Gabby and her family are
welcomed by us all, who know she is joining
Oscar, Francesca, Olivia and Simon in a beautiful,
loving family. I salute you all and I will end by
reciting a poem.

I cannot now recall which poem I recited but all went well and Oscar and Gabby are the grooviest couple in Brooklyn.

79

Dissing the Teletubbies

Stick thin, dressed all in black, with big hair and dark glasses, he exuded a wild rock-star glamour before he opened his mouth and the scintillating low-life couplets poured out of him. I became an instant fan of John Cooper Clarke from the moment I saw him and a few years later was honoured to spend a memorable afternoon watching the FA Cup Final with him before we shared the bill in some woodland-clearing show.

I was deeply under his influence when I wrote the following poem, which is probably best delivered in his style – at breakneck speed in a Mancunian accent. In truth I bore no ill will towards the Teletubbies when they first appeared on children's TV, but vitriol was the easiest emotion to employ in this tribute to John...

Tinky Winky, Dipsy, Laa-Laa and Po,
What the hell's goin' on in your terrible show?
You ponce around your green grassy humps
Like bloody great colourful gormless lumps.
You're always so happy, you never get sad,
You never feel crappy or do something bad.
You've got no problems, you never go gaga
Dipsy, Po, Tinky Winky and Laa-Laa.

Dipsy, Po, Tinky Winky and Laa-Laa,
I suppose you must think you're going quite far far,
But you're stuck in a ghetto, take it from me,
There's really no future in kiddies TV.
Each of you is nought but a harmless freak,
You'll never be asked onto *Start the Week*.
So come on, you softies, acquire some bad habits,
Get off yer arses and kidnap those rabbits,
Do something exciting, run away with a gypsy,
Po, Tinky Winky, Laa-Laa and Dipsy.

Po, Tinky Winky, Laa-Laa and Dipsy,
You've got no shoulders, you're entirely hipsy,
And Oi, Tipsy Dipsy, you must be the worst,
Your name would imply some terrible thirst.
There ought to be cells in the brain you lack,
Cos Dipsy stands for dipsomaniac.
But you'll never be caught having a drinky
Or smoking a spliff with Tinky the Winky.

Po, Dipsy, Laa-Laa and Tinky Winky,
Lose the fresh air and try living stinky,
Find Basil Brush and do something kinky,
Make breakfast from Perky and marmelise Pinky,
Cos life's not so easy, it can't be all love,
Look at the misery falling down from above.
Don't ponce around like some airhead lummox,
Rip those stupid TVs from your stomachs.
Come on Teletubs, give it a go,
Tinky Winky, Dipsy, Laa-Laa and Po,
Tinky Winky, Dipsy, Laa-Laa and Po.

80

Smoking

As you read this, if I am not dead, then I have definitely given up smoking and, if I am dead and still smoking, well that's another story. I am planning to go and stand in the garden and have a fag once I have finished writing this first paragraph. Of course, I am aware that it is stupid to smoke – especially if, like me, you have diabetes, but, godammit, nicotine is *SO* more-ish. My numerous falls from the smoke-free wagon shame me but I am definitely stopping forever *very* soon.

… Ahhh, that's better.

I took up smoking when I lived in Paris because not to have a *Gauloises sans-filtre* stuck in your mouth at all times seemed like an insult to the Parisians around me. I intended to drop the habit once I returned to Norwich and, indeed, I did stop smoking cigarettes – but only because I took up the cheaper option of rolling tobacco. I sought validation for my habit in the quotes of others I admired: 'The alternative is not immortality,' said Tom Stoppard. I took solace in the French composer Erik Satie's quote: 'My doctor told me, "Always smoke, my friend – if you do not, another will be smoking in your place."' And then there was the great writer Dennis Potter's eulogy to the 'cylinders of delight' and his assertation that he couldn't write anything without chain-smoking.

I have long suggested to friends, not entirely playfully, that I should set up a charity called 'Fags for homeless people.' I frequently offer a smoke (and some change) to the poor people sleeping rough and two of the biggest smiles I have ever seen leapt onto the faces of the pair of homeless guys in Glasgow to whom I once donated a whole packet of Marlboro Green.

I think my consistent failure to stop smoking derives from some fantasy vision of myself as a self-destructive romantic like Samuel Coleridge, or perhaps it is a kind of tribute to my father who, despite my mother's attempts to reform him, never managed to give up the fags for long. Besides, the joy of lighting up a cigarette outside the airport after a long-haul flight is delicious in a way no other experience can compare with (for about two seconds).

However, I am DEFINITELY giving up very soon, once I learn how to do the vape. See you on the pavement outside the restaurant.

81

The Oldest Cup
in the Cupboard

I am the oldest cup in this cupboard although there is one older one who lives in the ceramics cupboard higher up on the wall. Lady Blue we call her, because she wears a blue squiggly dress, tapers down and has her own saucer to stand on.

On the day I arrived here, as sunlight fell on me for the first time, paper was torn from me and there was human noise. I was placed on a surface and inspected. I had a shiny new white coat back then, displaying a yellow shield, above which, written in blue, was the legend 'Wimbledon FC'.

Soon, boiling tea filled me up and oh, I was thrilled by the heat and delighted that my handle stayed cold. It felt good to have started work so soon. I went back and forth to the human mouth. I met Starx the wine glass, who later joined me for a warm, greasy roll around the washing-up bowl before an upside-down stand together on the metal wrinkles of the draining board. By the time we went into our separate cupboards, Starx and I were firm friends. Sadly, a smashing sound that night meant that I never saw him again.

There were six other cups in our cupboard back then. I was respectful to the others, three of whom were the same shape as me, plus Nomay, who was fat, with two handles and a flower painted on his tummy, and Milly, who, being a pint mug, was bigger than the rest of us.

We all got along fine until that terrible day when everything changed…

I know you are now on tenterhooks (whatever they are), desperate to find out what this big plot-changing event might be and what becomes of all the cups. Watch out for The Oldest Cup in the Cupboard *on a bookshelf near you soon.*

82

How to Be an Alternative Tour Guide

Are you a starving actor or comic stuck miserably in the provinces with no work? Then read to the end of this and consider the possibility of earning money from showing off and having a laugh – with a guaranteed appearance on your local TV station.

But first, some background. In the mid-1980s in Edinburgh one year I decided to experiment with becoming a tour guide with a difference, the difference being that everything I told my audience was a fabrication in search of a laugh. The tours were free so, despite a minimal advertising campaign, there were always a dozen or so tourists for me to lead a dance down the Royal Mile.

As we proceeded along the famous road, I informed them that Edinburgh Castle was, in fact, a replica built in 1970; that the headless dummies in a shop window were the cast of the Oxford Revue company; that the flat at the top of one of the tenement buildings on the Mile had once been shared by Mary, Queen of Scots, Billy Connolly and Lulu; and that St Giles' Cathedral was made of cardboard. I disclosed the old by-law which meant we must all crawl the next 20 yards.

If a man in a kilt was walking by I might declare him to be the great-grandson of Robert the Bruce. More often than not, in the freewheeling festival atmosphere, the Scotsman in question would smile and answer questions on his heroic forebear. As we all ignored the beautiful old Tron Kirk, I revealed instead the glorious history of the Portakabin next to it. I climbed on top of a bus shelter for no reason and invited my audience to stand in a bin with me to experience how the city felt and smelt in the days of 'Auld Reekie.'

Occasionally I roped in fellow performers, persuading them to portray characters such as a mermaid washing her hair, who I claimed to be the mother of the Loch Ness monster, and an opera singer who bellowed Verdi tunefully from a high window. The audiences all seemed to have fun once they realised the nature of the tour and, given the ticket price, they were definitely getting value for money.

So, young performer, I propose that you immediately rise from your couch of melancholy and become another alternative tour guide. The ideal place for this venture is a city frequented by tourists – Exeter, Norwich, York, Oxford, Dundee, Winchester, Venice, etc – but, with an appropriate act, you could do it anywhere that people gather and, if you want to get yourself a grant, describe your tour as 'immersive, site-specific, promenade-performance art'.

Tailor the walk to suit your own talent, wear a wig or a Batman costume, get your friends to jump out from behind corners and windows. Soon you can take a hat round at the end or start charging a fiver.

I wish you well and hope you sprinkle the streets with laughter. I seek no thanks for this advice but feel free to send me some cash in a brown envelope.

83

PC Syd's Painful Night

Here is another small slice from my dad's memoir in which he suffers badly, but now he is not a soldier but PC Syd Smith of the London Metropolitan Police, Kennington branch. We, his sons, were always excited when we heard his key in the door as we ate breakfast, knowing he had come back from a long night on the beat. He would kiss my mother, remove his uniform jacket, unclip the collar on his blue lined police shirt, light a fag and then join us in a bowl of Ready Brek. He never told us how his night had gone and we never asked, which, given the following story, is probably for the best.

> *My worst experience occurred at 10.30pm outside the Old Vic in Waterloo Road. I was about to go off duty. People were coming out of the theatre. Opposite the theatre was a car park and men were about to get on a coach. A young lady was walking past. The men started shouting rude remarks to her to which she told them, in no uncertain manner, to fuck off. I remonstrated with the men and also suggested to the young lady that she ignore them and carry on her way. She promptly told me that I could fuck off as well. The men*

stopped their shouting but she persisted in swearing and berating them. In the meantime a crowd had gathered and were obviously enjoying the proceedings, probably more than they had 'The Midsummer Night's Dream'. I had to do something more practicable to prevent a further breach of the peace. I told her that if she persisted I would have to arrest her. She replied 'Well, fucking well arrest me then.'

I couldn't lose face so I attempted to arrest her. With that an unholy struggle took place. I grabbed her arm and in the melée she fell to the ground, and she reached up and gripped my testicles and then bit my leg through my trousers. Each time I tried to get her to her feet she just twisted the former. A passing policeman going off duty to Edward Henry police flats enquired if I was alright, which seemed to me a bloody stupid enquiry. I suggested he phoned for the black maria and assistance.

After a long and painful time a police car and a van arrived. The driver got out and he managed to get her to her feet and with that she promptly kicked him in the crotch. He was a Scot with a known short fuse and he was just about to draw her off one when he became aware of the crowd and thought better of it. It eventually took 5 officers to get her in the van and back to the

*station. The divisional surgeon had to be called to
treat my bite, which had drawn blood. And
because of that I had to charge her with 'assault on
police'. That was the only time I had ever charged
anyone with that offence.*

*At Tower Bridge Court the following morning the
young lady pleaded guilty to the charge in front of
Miss Campbell, the only female Stipendiary
Magistrate. The girl was given a conditional
discharge although she had numerous convictions
for assault on police and prostitution.*

I feel my father's pain here but I also have sympathy for
the woman who caused it, as I suspect he did, too. The
Scottish cop was out of order as who knows what hard
background she came from. Although he was a
policeman, Syd never really wanted to arrest anybody
unless they needed a cell roof for the night, but I guess if
you are being chewed to death and having your bollocks
squeezed you might need to take whatever action you can.

84

Losing It

A friend once remarked of me, 'He is not good with things.' Anyone who spends time in my company soon learns of my tendency to break things, manhandle them, drop them and, almost certainly, lose them. If everything I have ever lost was gathered together in one place I would need a space the size of a castle to house it all. This castle would be rammed to the ramparts with jumpers, shirts, socks, a sufficient number of scarves to make a belt to wrap around the world and gloves to warm the hands of a small army. There would be credit cards, books, packets of cigarettes, phones, hundreds of pairs of glasses and enough cash to keep me going for at least 15 years.

Perhaps I have a condition related to ADHD or dyspraxia or the opposite of OCD, whatever that may be. I have certainly always been like this and have to factor in the possibility that anything I own (apart from my home) may one day end up without me on a train, a bench, in a hotel or in the bowels of some sundry lost-property department. My family, old girlfriends, former flatmates and Beth have had to learn to cope with my disarray and I thank them all for so doing, especially Beth, who despite my chaotic ways, has tolerated me for 20 years.

When I lose something (which happens most days) I like to console myself with the thought that whoever has found it is a worthy recipient. I once had a brilliant comedy stage outfit that had a huge mouth stuck on the front of a black body-stocking with a big cigarette sticking comically out of the red lips. I had commissioned a fashion student to make it, so it was unique. Of course, I ended up leaving it in its bag at a venue I was playing one night. My disappointment at this loss was, however, transformed into delight when, years later, a woman told me that she had seen a man wearing it at a Gay Pride march in Madrid. *Hurra por los manifestantes gays de Madrid!*

Sometimes I wonder who got the coat. Parroting a mantra of her grandma's, 'A good coat will take you anywhere,' Beth persuaded me to splash out on a bottle-green cashmere overcoat from a posh shop, because, 'It doesn't matter then how scruffy you are underneath.' It was beautiful – for the four days I had it. Then I left it on the luggage rack of a train heading to Huddersfield. We rang all the branches of the Lost Property section of TransPennine to no avail.

I didn't lose the coat, the coat lost me. I like to think that the person who found it was having a terrible time of it that cold, December day and had never had a warm coat, until they found this one. My warmest of wishes are extended to whosoever you may be. And my thanks to Beth's dear friend Pauline who sent me a new scarf in sympathy, which survived all winter before it left me for a chair outside a cafe.

85

An Unusual Date

One of the consolations of growing older is that you are more likely to be coupled up and therefore less likely to go on dates anymore. In these 'swipe left' online times, getting a date is easier but the actual 'meeting-up-for-the-first-time' game seems unchanged.

'What is the worst date you've ever been on?' is a question which is likely to produce some grimly hilarious stories. I heard from my friend about the man who was so boring on the subject of his previous girlfriend on his first date with her that she went to the toilet from where she escaped out the back entrance, leaving him with two dinners seasoned with the pity of the waiter. I've had a few disasters myself, including the occasion where my date disappeared for 20 minutes to have sex with another man in the toilet.

I met Diane very briefly at a party and within half an hour we had shared a kiss. I gave her my number and next day she rang and invited me to her place in Brixton that evening. This seemed very promising. She answered the door to her small basement flat looking fresh and beautiful, and welcomed me in with a smile. And this is where it began to go wrong.

Diane introduced me to Lee, a small young man in a checked shirt who was sitting on the floor, cross-legged, wearing thin glasses and an expression that said, 'Why have you brought this horrible man round?' It became apparent very swiftly that Lee was besotted with Diane, who in turn treated him like a small puppy. She disappeared into the kitchen to open the wine I had brought, whereupon Lee embarked on a lengthy speech about various bands I had never heard of. Diane returned and he sat at her feet, gazing up at her, which I soon saw she liked very much indeed.

'Shall we put some music on?' I said.

'I don't have any,' said Diane, 'but let's play my answerphone messages.'

And so she did. The messages were unremarkable, inaudible or just silent and the evening was becoming distinctly odd. I announced I was suddenly feeling a bit ill and started to leave, at which point Diane despatched the obedient Lee into the kitchen and sat down next to me. She then lowered her eyes and paused before whispering, 'There's something I need to tell you...'

She breathed heavily. I waited. She looked up at me.

'Two months ago,' she paused, 'I was kidnapped by aliens who took me into space and made me have sex with them...'

I found it very hard to know how to respond to this.

'And do you know what? I really enjoyed it. It was the best time of my life.'

I made a noise somewhere between a gasp of horror and a yelp of laughter. She looked at me seductively but I held my nerve and told her I now had a headache too and I'm sorry, I must go. As I left I nodded at Lee, who was looking much happier than when I arrived.

I have told this story many times but in recent years I have come to see Diane not as a laughable vixen but, rather, as a woman with mental health issues. I hope wherever she is, she is OK now.

Or maybe it was some elaborate role-play that I had failed to fathom? Was Lee a part of it? Or perhaps sex in space with aliens is a real thing and the panacea we all need. In which case, see you tomorrow night between Saturn and Uranus.

86

Wrestling with Phones

In 2002, following my flirtation with death, I set off on a long, convalescent solo ramble round my beloved Cornish coast path, walking gently along the cliffs and stopping overnight at humble B&Bs (long before the word 'Air' got in front of them). Concerned that I might topple off a rock into the waves and no one would notice me, my dear Beth bought me my first ever mobile phone.

I didn't fall into the sea but, unfortunately, the phone did. I confessed to Beth that evening from a phone box and went another year unmobilised until it became apparent that, without one, I would probably never work again. 'What do you mean you can't contact him? Hasn't he got a mobile?'

My next clunky grey phone served me well, happy to just nestle in my pocket bleeping sporadically and feeling no need to come on holiday with us. After it chose to stay on a train I had got off, I bought one that wanted to be a BlackBerry. And finally, of course, again encouraged by Beth, I became one of the 700 million people who own an iPhone.

No doubt I have the settings wrong but the thin shiny oblong, which makes me think of a tiny gravestone, seems to demand constant attention and never ceases to suggest bleepy ways it can help me:

Coo-eee! Come on Arthur, look at me! Why don't I pay all your bills, answer any question you can think of, put you in touch with everyone in the world, tell you where you're going, take over your bank account, be your train ticket?

And – emoji – do you want to hang out with me and some of my pals? There's loads of us – Twitter, Wiki, WhatsApp, Uber, Viber, Deliveroo, Siri – they're a right laugh! Look, they're here, waiting for you!

And, by the way, pensioners in Balham are going mad for this new type of hearing aid.

Oh, hang on, I need charging. Charge me Arthur, there are no chargers where you're going and come on, you can't go without me! I've gone red, I'm down to 10 per cent!

You might conclude from all this that I am a grumpy old man who will never get a booking in Silicon Valley and whose algorithms date from so far back I still put letters in postboxes. It is true; I am suspicious of my phone's ability to tell the world where I am at any given moment, and of its desire to learn everything about me. I am also trying to resist becoming one of those people who sits opposite you in the restaurant, silently gazing at their wrist. And yet... and yet...

I *do* want to send Beth a funny picture of where I am; I want to post a gag to my rambling WhatsApp pals; see if anyone has replied to my tweet; work out if it's left or right at the top of the road... oh dear, it's happened. I shall continue to refuse to learn *all* its tricks and resist its infinite offerings but I now realise that I have joined the hundreds of millions of humans who would feel lost without this scary new magic lantern that wants to own us all.

87

Art for Comedy's Sake

The following is the transcript of the speech I made at my recent interview for the post of Emeritus Professor of Artism at the Slade School of Artiness:

We do not think of comedy and art as being related or, if they are, it is at several removes. In all paintings and sculptures from medieval times up to the Renaissance and beyond, there is nothing much amusing. The most you can find is the odd peasant in a Fra Angelico crowd scene pointing the wrong way, or in one or two of the *Last Suppers* I have seen there are some comical haircuts, but, for the art lover looking for a chuckle to relieve the diet of religious pain and martyrdom, there is sod all.

The Sistine Chapel is an awesome sight – but laughs? Nothing. Zilch. The Cavalier may be laughing but I'm not. Look at those Modigliani paintings – why the long faces?

Classical artists were at least prepared to go for the odd smutty snigger; there is a depiction of the great Priapus, the Greek god of fertility, weighing his own enormous erection which always raises a smile, while the old Pan-having-sex-with-a-goat statue retrieved at Pompei would certainly entertain a Comedy Store crowd for a few minutes. But even the ancients tended to save comedy for plays or festivals.

This was the case until 1917 when the French artist Marcel Duchamp unveiled what had been voted by experts (real ones – not just ones I've made up to suit my purposes) 'the most influential art work of the 20th century.' Titled *Fountain*, it is an ordinary men's urinal which Duchamp altered crucially by signing the name R. Mutt on the side. This is of course, a gag, one might even say a representation of the phrase 'taking the piss.' However, the art critics, lacking any sense of humour, raised it into a work of colossal significance and so it has remained.

The Dadaists were a bunch of comedy artists (among them Duchamp) who reacted against the stupid, grim slaughter of the First World War by being absurd, ridiculous and provocative. All the certainties about Art that had existed before were questioned, laughed at and pissed on. And so Alternative Comedy was born and I... Pardon? No, I've got another 10 pages of this... how dare you! Come back! Well, if that's your attitude I'm going. Good day to you.

Still haven't heard if I got the job at the Slade.

88

Nearly 90

At the care home Mum is sitting in the main lounge among her fellow residents, softly singing along to Frank Sinatra's *Fly Me to the Moon*, one of the repertoire of songs from the 1940s and 1950s that flow throughout the day from the speaker in the corner. I recall my father telling me that Sinatra was Hazel's teenage 'pash' and observe again how calming music can be for people with dementia. A jolly guitarist called Paul comes to the home every week and leads a singalong of old tunes and, when I have attended these sessions with Hazel, I am always surprised to see how residents who are otherwise permanently silent often mouth along the words.

'Hello Mother!' She is always delighted to see us but sometimes she forgets who we are. A few weeks ago she asked me, 'And how are your parents?' This is a kind of comfort to me since it suggests she does not need me as much as she once did.

Beth and I take Hazel to her small, clean room, with its en-suite bathroom and glass back door giving on to a communal garden. Beth helps her into her coat and we shuffle along the corridor to the door of the dementia wing. A young carer comes running to let us out and, when I thank him, he says, 'Hazel is my mother.' Then he looks embarrassed, perhaps fearful that I might be offended. 'She is my mother too,' I smile, 'so we must be brothers.' We shake hands as bros. The carers here are from all over the world but share a kindness and a dedication to their job that fills me with admiration.

We head over to the garden a short way beyond the home, which is tended by some of the patients from Springfield Hospital, and plonk ourselves down on the familiar bench, which sits within a wooden frame wrapped in roses, overlooking pretty flowerbeds. There was a time when my mother could have named all of these flowers. 'Look, the sun is just going down,' she exclaims, 'and look at all the leaves!'

From my wallet I produce an old photo in which Hazel immediately identifies herself, her sister and brother on the day of their evacuation during the War. On the back, handwritten in ink, is the date, September 1939. I ask Hazel to spell 'successfully', which she does successfully, and then point out that it is one of only two words in the English language which contain three sets of double letters. 'Can you think of the other word?' I ask her, hoping for the answer 'committee' but she floors me with 'Unsuccessfully?'

Beth shows Hazel her new watch, which she studies closely with intense pleasure. I read out a poem by T S Eliot, whose work she once knew and adored. It was Hazel taking her young sons to plays and encouraging us to read novels that gave me the taste for words that led me to my profession. She is attentive throughout my reading of 'The Love Song of J Alfred Prufrock', enjoying the journey of the words, if no longer, perhaps, their full meaning.

There is a radiant pink sky as we head back the 150 yards to the care home. Having lived here for six years, she is now a senior resident, known to all. She has become a little wobblier, but her decline is slow compared to other residents, who may go from lively confusion to seated silence to death within a year. Sometimes I wonder if I'll catch up with her and have to move in next door. Ho hum. At the door to the home I slip away and Beth takes her back to Frank Sinatra.

As Beth and I walk home through the leaves I think of all the people I know who are in states of despair over betrayals, illnesses and deaths. Being with my mother now is to enter a world where all the harsh jangling of daily life seems quietened and softened. She has attained a kind of grace, for which I am deeply thankful.

89

Saturday in Athens

In London there are numerous buildings competing to be the one on the front of the guidebooks – St Paul's Cathedral, Tower Bridge, Buckingham Palace, Nelson's Column and, Johnny-come-lately, the Shard.

Other cities have only one truly iconic landmark. In Paris it is the Eiffel Tower, in Barcelona the Sagrada Familia, in Sydney it is the Opera House – all splendid structures no doubt, but none of them compare with the iconic dominatrix of the capital of ancient and modern Greece.

You can just discern her, a faded imprint
In the matinal shimmer,
A little shabbier than one might hope
She sits and thinks and sits and thinks
About her glorious heyday years
(which all the world is still applauding)
And wonders what will become of her...

But then, as dusk unfolds,
She starts to sparkle and pout and glow
And all the lights way down below
Salute their boss
In her moonlit gloss.

As midnight comes
She starts to preen
And feel the joy of what she's been.
From her columns, centuries spill,
Shining, shining on her ancient hill.
'Hey all yous,' she suddenly cries,
'All you lot beneath the skies,
Who on earth do you think you are?
Round Athens way there's just one star.
Everybody suck on this –
I am the fucking Acropolis.'

13 September 2014 – Athens

90

Sleeping with Lord Nelson (and Others)

As a TV presenter I have fronted some very boring items – you may well have forgotten my piece on loft extensions on whatever that programme was called from ages ago – but I have also been despatched to some wonderful places.

I did a series of four-minute films for BBC's *The One Show* called 'Sleeping with…' in which I spent the night at the house of a range of historical figures, including George Bernard Shaw, Florence Nightingale, Benjamin Disraeli, Rudyard Kipling and George Eliot. Most of these places are now National Trust properties containing artefacts and memorabilia relating to their former residents and each creates a portrait of a life and its times.

At Lord Byron's ancestral home at the former priory known as Newstead Abbey in Nottinghamshire I enjoyed a drink from the cup he had had fashioned from a skull; in Beatrix Potter's house in the Lake District I laughed to hear an American tourist ask if Beatrix was Harry Potter's grandmother. At the house in Hampstead where Sigmund Freud and his daughter Anna lived after fleeing Nazi Austria, I sneakily had a lie down on what is probably the most famous couch in the world.

After a day spent telling the story of my subject, interviewing experts about them and how they came to this residence, I would have dinner with the TV crew before bedding down in a camp bed somewhere on the property. As you can imagine, these were not humble dwellings and lying alone in some enormous Victorian room could feel strange and spooky but I did feel a proximity to these big characters from the past that I may not have experienced in the local Travelodge.

At the sculptor Henry Moore's house in Hertfordshire I couldn't sleep, so, in the middle of the night, I walked out under the stars and stared at the big stone sculpted creatures in the huge garden. At Agatha Christie's beautiful home in Devon I sat at 2am on a bench in her private wood and looked down at the distant lights on the River Dart. At the Brontës' parsonage in Haworth, West Riding, I watched snow falling outside and contemplated those three brilliant writer sisters and their drunken artist brother who lived there together with their father, an Irish Anglican priest. All of the children died before their father, whose grief one can only imagine.

My nocturnal excursions were solitary affairs apart from one scary time when I nearly got arrested near the world's most famous warship, HMS *Victory*. Lying next to Lord Nelson's small bunk bed, imagining the sway of the seas, I found I needed a pee at 3am. There was no toilet available on the ship (maybe they just poured it overboard?) so I had to walk across a concrete courtyard to a Portakabin loo.

Halfway there the silence was ruptured by the sound of three black cars screeching to a halt around me. Three uniformed drivers got out and looked at me very severely. 'What are you doing here?' one of them asked sternly. At this point I remembered that this was a military dockyard and a man wandering around it in the middle of the night in his pyjamas needed to explain himself.

I doubt any terrorist has attempted to avoid arrest by claiming he was doing something for *The One Show*; it sounded so unlikely that they must have realised it was genuine and, after one of the military policemen radioed through to someone who confirmed my story, I was allowed to go on my way. I relieved myself in a state of some relief. I didn't mention this incident in my 'piece to camera' next morning and I enjoyed a very deep sleep back at home that afternoon.

My thanks to the BBC for allowing me these dreamy nights and my apologies for that time I called *The One Show* '*Blue Peter* for grown-ups.'

91

Oh What a Day
That Will Be

This was a poem I wrote in the mid-1980s to perform at a show in a pub full of left-wingers in Islington. Its strident tone is not one I would adopt these days but I offer it as a small portrait of another time when politics divided the nation, when AIDS was spreading, the Cold War was still a thing and young men like me were ANGRY.

When the Tories are out and Margaret's a goner,
And Wimbledon FC buy Diego Maradona,
When they arrest the Queen and drugs
   are found on her,
Oh what a day that will be.

When Murdoch's riches are converted to rags,
When you don't die young from smoking fags,
And we all have the chance of afternoon shags,
Oh what a day that will be.

When the worst you can get is a dose of the clap,
The day Palestine appears on a map.
When Jeffrey Archer says, 'What I write is crap',
Oh what a day that will be.

When being black is no longer a crime,
And the condom slides on (pop) first time,
And when Nigel Lawson crawls back to
    the slime,
Oh what a day that will be.

When the Berlin Wall has got no bricks,
And when men don't measure the size
    of their dicks,
When Sylvester Stallone weighs seven stone six,
Oh what a day that will be.

When High Court judges don't
    countenance rape,
And we're not so tight-arsed that a fart
    can't escape,
Then it's time for Batman to hang up his cape,
Oh what a day that will be,
What a wonderful day that will be.

92

The Sweetest Blackberries

What is the finest, most delicious orange you ever ate? You don't know? Well, let me tell you about mine.

On holiday in Andalucia in southern Spain I had just woken from a brief but deeply satisfying siesta. Beth continued snoozing as I sauntered onto our little hotel balcony and gazed across rocky sands at the long, jagged silhouette of the Alpujarras mountains on the horizon. Then my eye was caught by a blazing circular thing in the foreground; sitting on a plate, left out for me by Beth. More or less shouting 'Eat me!' was a large orange, no doubt recently detached from one of the orange trees nearby. The peel easily fell away beneath my thumb and, within moments, the first segment had started an extravagant taste party in my mouth. It was the orangey-ist of all my oranges.

I have similar stories relating to my best ever cup of tea, my finest Diet Coke and my all-time top tomato. The perfect confluence of person, place, time and foodstuff is a rare occurrence and I am still waiting for the unbeatable pistachio nut, the greatest grape and the ultimate ice cream.

Another fruity epiphany came to me one September as I was walking along the sumptuous Devonian cliffs between Dartmouth and Salcombe on a glorious, warm afternoon. Having covered 10 miles or so I began to wilt and sweat beneath the hot sun. As a diabetic of years standing, I recognised that I was heading towards a hypo – my blood-sugar levels were way too low and, if I did not consume some form of sugar very soon, I may pass out and fall into a coma. No problem; I plunged my hand into my rucksack to retrieve the large bottle of sweet apple juice I had brought with me… but, oh dear, the wetness of my jumper told me I had made my old mistake – I didn't screw the top on the bottle properly. There was an empty bottle, sopping clothes but no apple juice.

I was swaying now like some roaming drunk and becoming fearful; the nearest shop was at least a mile away – would I make it that far? Probably not. And how long before anyone came along if I needed rescuing? I spotted a house on the brow of a hill and staggered towards it, hoping to find there a Samaritan with something saccharine, anything, but, as I dreamt my way uphill, it seemed to grow no closer. Maybe I needed a lie down…

And then I see them. Among the fading buds and bushes lining the path, there are a few gleaming blackberries that have ripened early. I fall upon them, grabbing at them in relief and, as I guzzle, I see more that are already in their prime, and then more. O goodness, they are exquisite! After gobbling several handfuls of the heavenly orbs, I feel stronger and my body returns to its normal (relatively) robust state – even if I am dribbling purple juice down my chin. Were I to live another 1,000 years I know that I shall never enjoy a feast of blackberries quite as much as those sweet, life-saving West Country beauties.

Heading through trees to the shop to replenish my supplies, I thought of my father who, having been a starving prisoner of war, could never resist the allure of free food and who had his own 'special place' in a field outside Bath which he visited every year to pick the new crop of blackberries, waiting there resplendent in their sparkling welcome. I walked on swathed in relief and contentment.

93

Travelling Man

One afternoon I was chatting to a barmaid in a pub in a village in Devon. We agreed she was lucky to live in such a pretty place. 'But sometimes,' I asked, 'don't you long for the bright lights? You're only young, wouldn't you like to feel the buzz of a big city?'

'Oh no,' she replied, 'I've been to Crediton – it was too fast for me there.'

Not everyone feels the urge to travel but, as a teenager, I was hungry to taste foreign cultures, to find out if they really *did* speak French in France. I spent a good part of my 20s stuck somewhere very far away and very hot, gesticulating uselessly to a man with a moustache and a polite smile. I slept in run-down hostels, soggy tents, and on beaches hosting mosquito parties. It was wild.

Eventually my circumstances, and therefore my travel arrangements, improved and now, if you wish, I can show you umpteen blurred holiday snaps of me in exotic places around the world. (Oh, would you rather not?).

In recent years, however, the itching in my feet and my wanderlust have softened. When I am sitting in my garden and see a plane passing overhead, I do not wriggle with jealousy; I am, rather, thankful *not* to be sitting in that tin deathtrap en route to some distant hellhole. If someone told me I shall never fly again, I would accept it and congratulate myself on my contribution to the fight against global warming.

You can't *go everywhere*. There are more towns, mountains and beaches in the world than there are hours in a life and, frankly, can't I just stay home and watch something on Netflix with Beth? Walking in the Himalayas? Sounds good but I'll take a turn around the common first if you don't mind. I have had a sunburnt bellyful of cramped aeroplanes, misconceived food orders and wet afternoons trying to be jolly under trying circumstances. I am done standing in the wrong queue, wincing at the local liqueur and trying to pilot a pedalo with a hangover.

Good luck to all you romantic wanderers but I find there are always, if I wish, new places to visit that are more easily accessible.

Like Crediton in Devon – I hear it's rather lively there.

PS Even as I typed the stay-at-home words above I found myself thinking, yes, but I'd *love* to see Japan some day… Hmmmm… be nice to join my American pal at the New Orleans jazz fest… and Lisbon – how come I've never been there? It's not a long flight. I'll see if Beth fancies a weekend break. Gosh, it would be good to get a booking at that comedy club in Singapore… My wanderlust will never disappear entirely, I suspect.

94

It's Late September

The end of summer and the sun was flowing across the concrete campus of the University of East Anglia on the outskirts of Norwich, where I was a student in the mid-1970s. It's late September and I really was back at school, not to study Comparative Literature this time but to take part in the celebrations for the university's 50th birthday.

There was a plethora of groovy activities – a big top featuring Kid Creole and the Coconuts on a bill with former student, now ground-breaking ventriloquist Nina Conti, a funfair, some serious academic lectures and discussions, an unexpected invasion of zombies, a firework volcano and umpteen eclectic performances in every genre.

When not joining in with all this, grizzled old alumnae like me got to hang out in old haunts with dimly remembered contemporaries and to smile in wistful wonder at the current crop of undergrads resplendent in their youthful zeal.

My duties at the University Theatre (a patch of grass when I was a student) were to perform a 50-minute comedy set and, far more taxing, to play the main character in an extract from Samuel Beckett's play *Fin de*

Partie (in English *Endgame*). As an ardent admirer of Beckett's plays I had readily agreed to this suggestion without considering if I was really capable of it...

The director, Professor Emeritus Ralph Yarrow, and fellow (bilingual) actor Erwann Limon, helped me through a rehearsal the night before, at the end of which it was agreed I could read my part. My French is likely better than yours but I have hardly spoken it in recent years and learning a long script in the language was too much. I went to sleep drenched in apprehension and spent the day studying the text of the play and practising my pronunciations.

There are four characters in *Fin de Partie* and, this being Beckett, two of them have no legs and live in dustbins. These two did not feature in our extract, in which I played Hamm, a hunched, sickly man in a wheelchair who, although blind, was (in our version) able to read the script in front of him. When the time came, I was wheeled on stage by Erwann, playing the part of my servant Clov, and we began the dialogue. My French accent slowly improved as we proceeded and Erwann's excellent timing won us several laughs. We were doing well until I turned over too many pages and lost my place...

The audience could see I was in trouble so I ad-libbed in a way I felt appropriate to Beckett (in French, *bien sûr*, but I translate):

'I have arrived at the wrong page. This page means nothing to me now. Where is the right page? I look and look for the right page but it has gone. It is lost. I am lost. No, wait, the right page is found!'

The audience laughed. By now I was beginning to remember the French flourishes I had adopted during my year in Paris. The corners of my mouth began to droop and my shoulders arched into that gallic shape. *Alors, quoi?*

Erwann and I made it triumphantly through to the end. I was thrilled to have got away with it, and it reminded me that doing something unfamiliar provides a bigger buzz than doing what you know.

And then I bumped into one of comedy's true originals, the great Eddie Izzard. Eddie has an honorary degree from UEA and was performing his French stand-up show in half an hour's time. We reminisced in French together before Eddie invited me to do a spot to introduce him. And so, as I once did in Paris 20 years ago, I cracked gags in French and, still fired up by my debut as a French actor, *je me suis bien amusé.*

Afterwards I took my place among the throng of students past and present who were draped on the steps overlooking the square at the centre of the campus. I smoked a fag and reflected that I had first sat here 40 years ago, an excited fresher, newly departed from the nest, hungry for fresh ideas and experiences. Whatever happened to him? He is still inside me somewhere, I hope.

My musings were interrupted by the arrival of two attractive undergrad women who sat down and flirted with me for as long as it took to cadge two cigarettes (about 20 seconds), at which point they immediately got up and set off towards the bar. I smiled, gathered my stuff, waved goodbye to my 20-year-old self and set off back home to London town.

95

Easy Smuggling

It was only half an hour since I had taken up my new career in crime but, as I returned from my secret assignation in the old port of Wells-next-the-Sea, I was already enjoying myself hugely. I was out and about with a company who organise a range of activities on the north Norfolk coast, including fishing, foraging, wild swimming, sailing, rowing, and – my own choice – smuggling. Or as it said in the brochure, 'Taking an advanced adventurous sail which provides a training and preparation phase on traditional smuggling techniques in old sailing boats before running an actual operation.'

Thus inspired by the thought of the millions to be made from untaxed goods plus a bit of sailing, I found myself in Wells-next-the-Sea (NB Do NOT insert a 'to' between 'next' and 'the' or you will be run out of town), a small, charming port in that salty green coastal mush of Norfolk where land meets sea and they dance together among the waterways, arcade shops, chippies, fishing boats and seafood stalls.

Waiting on the quayside for me was Henry, a former marine and a charmer to boot, who was to be my mentor in the art of trafficking. Henry told me about the smugglers of yore who brought in goods from all over Europe, making huge profits from the duties they avoided.

How did they do this? Henry smiled and told me the name of a coffee house nearby where I must now go to 'pick up a message'.

As I entered the dark cafe I was feeling nervous and shifty. Was I being watched? Henry had told me to make contact with a man who 'looks like a smuggler' but having never knowingly met a smuggler I had no idea what this might mean. A furtive glance revealed a man with a beard sipping a coffee. I realised he looked *exactly* like a smuggler. I walked over to him. 'Are you Steve the smuggler?'

After a chat with Steve, who surreptitiously slipped a piece of paper in my pocket, I reported back to Henry. We looked at Steve's message, which gave six numbers and said '10 yards SW'. The numbers were a grid reference to a location nearby, so it was all aboard Henry's small blue boat and off into the swirling mass of muddy channels that lay between us and the open sea. I was rather smug that I hadn't needed Henry's help to decipher the grid reference. I learned that if we had been out at night he could have shown me how to navigate by the stars.

It was high tide but, even so, manoeuvring the boat through the watery channels required great expertise. Henry was helped by able seaman Paul, who bravely waded through the mud, pushing the boat round until we reached the exact grid point and, sure enough, there was the contraband – a solitary bottle of brandy, placed at this spot, presumably, by a dodgy smuggling pal of Steve's from abroad. In the 18th century there would have been many more bottles but I was content with one.

We turned around, I ducked again to avoid the sail and we mooched off back to Wells where, fingers crossed, the police were not lying in wait and we could flog off our bottle for a profit.

It was another afternoon indulging in ludicrous pursuits in East Anglia. I hope I have a few more left and that, in the meantime, I keep clear of undercover customs officers.

96

And If By Chance

And if by chance it happens
That I drop dead in a row,
In a standard-issue dispute
Like the one we're having now,

Then please do not imagine
This moment weighed an ounce;
I know that you still love me,
Even in your perfect flounce.

97

Mindlessness

You have a decent job that you enjoy, no serious medical problems, enough money to be going on with, a home, a loving family and friends and spring is a-coming. And yet, and yet… And yet you are as miserable as hell.

In recent years we have become more aware that mental health problems can be as bad for you as any physical condition. Yet the ways of dealing with them are less clear and more various. Here are just a few of the types of therapy that author, comedian and depressive Ariane Sherine tried in her excellent book *Talk Yourself Better*: psychodynamic, integrative, cognitive behavioural, cognitive analytic, gestalt, hypnotherapy, psychoanalysis, and on and on. And, of course, every religion has some prayerful guidance to overcoming despair and achieving contentment, even if you may have to wait until you die before this becomes possible.

And then there was the new kid on the therapy block, 'mindfulness', which threatened to overwhelm all the others. As this bandwagon rolled by I leapt on sceptically and presented a satire called *Mindlessness – A Beginner's Course* at the Edinburgh Fringe. This was my publicity schtick:

My course is for all those who fear their spiritual
journey may involve 'bus replacement' or who
can't be bothered to get up early for yoga;
who would rather be having a coffee and
reading the paper than chanting naked up
a mountain, or who don't feel they need to
go on a 6-week retreat in order to learn
how to breathe.

With the aid of my clever friend Jon King, I set up the Daphne Fairfax Mindlessness website, which contained short films of me towel-folding, colouring in and stroking socks. They are still on YouTube should you feel the need to relax your way out of your despair but, be warned, these therapies don't always go to plan...

On stage I dispensed earnest clichés sprinkled in inspirational quotes with added punchlines:

The magic in your life is inside you – but it can be
taken out with a simple surgical procedure.

Hug often and you'll get comfort when you need it.
Hug too often and you'll get a restraining order.

Never stop talking or all is lost. Unless you are at
a funeral.

At least it is always summer under the armpits.

*When times are hard you find out who your real
friends are. They're OK, but not as good as your
imaginary ones.*

*Keep moving forward – unless you are in a
rowing boat.*

*Realise that other people's pain is as great as your
own. On the other hand, who cares about your
dead dad – I've got a splinter and it really hurts!*

The show passed off reasonably well but I chose not to
perform it again after the Edinburgh run because I felt my
cynicism was rather harsh. Clearly, many people had
benefited from 'mindfulness' so who was I to decry it?

Nevertheless, I would submit that one way of coping
with one's troubles is to learn to laugh at them and at the
absurdity of being a big-brained, hairless biped lumbering
around in ignorance because, whatever your mental or
physical state, if you can take a little time out to laugh,
then you will feel a bit better, at last while the laugh lasts.

Whatever gets you through the night.

98

Another Disaster
That Didn't Happen

My late-night alternative tour of Edinburgh's Royal Mile is an annual event that, in my alcohol-soaked years, was routinely described as 'notorious' and once ended with my arrest for breach of the peace. However, the last tour of my boozing years could have had a far worse outcome than that and I still shudder to remember it.

At the junction of the Royal Mile and George IV Bridge there is a balustrade on which, on the night in question, I stood and addressed my motley followers. After informing them that The Proclaimers (whose song *I'm Gonna Be (500 Miles)* is the Scottish singalong of our age) started out as a Pinky and Perky tribute act, I offered a tenner to any man who would join me on the balustrade, take his top off and sing *Scotland the Brave*.

A guy duly took the cash, stepped up and belted out the song to raucous acclaim, after which I was heckled by a female audience member, 'Why didn't you offer a tenner for a woman to do it?' Fair enough – I duly offered her the cash, whereupon I stepped down as she climbed up, took off her top, swayed and sang with a gusto that is perhaps only possible at 3am in Edinburgh in August. Someone subsequently sent me a photograph of this and I am looking at it now. There she is, in her red bra, her dishevelled blonde hair blowing in the wind, her left hand waving her blouse, a huge smile covering her face and, in the background, people cheering her wildly.

Little did I know.

The next afternoon, as I was lugging my weighty hangover past this spot on the way to my last show of the festival, I looked again at the wall on which I and my volunteers had stood 10 hours earlier and froze in horror. Behind it was a drop of about 50 feet. If either of my two singers had toppled backwards from this precarious position – not at all unlikely given their level of intoxication – they would almost certainly have fallen to their deaths. The photograph of that brave woman at the height of the bacchanal would have depicted the last seconds of her life and no doubt would have ended up on some internet list of 'pictures taken moments before death'.

And, whether or not I was charged with manslaughter, I would have had to carry a burden of guilt for the rest of my life. I am so pleased that stupid, reckless, drunken man has become a stupid, rather less reckless, sober man. And, if you are the woman in question reading this and suddenly recalling that night, do get in touch and we'll have a cup of tea to celebrate the fact that we are both still alive.

99

I'm on the Train

I am well placed on the train (table to myself, perfect seat) to enjoy the flashes of coastline after Berwick. The hour of departure comes. And goes. 'Trouble with the locomotive,' says the guard. A woman with a loud baby sits opposite me. I take my newspaper out. I feel it coming and it does – we must change trains.

New train but continued delay. This is annoying.

A bullet smashed through her upper arm, her four brothers dead.

The guard comes through the carriage, 'Does this jacket belong to anyone?' The wait continues.

The men came at 6am. People ran from the village, the men were shooting them.

A woman snaps into her mobile, 'I don't know when I'll arrive. This train service is a shambles.' She is angry.

Helicopters circled overhead, they bombed the houses with hand grenades.

The train starts to move.

The death squads have come to West Darfur.

I put down the newspaper and settle into my seat.

100

Flamingos in the Bar

I had gone to a friend's place in the south of France intending to forget my broken heart by writing a comedy show for the Edinburgh Fringe. Arles, as occupied by the Romans and painted by Van Gogh, is an exquisite little town but, for three days, all I had done was to moon joylessly around the house sipping brandy. I felt little enthusiasm for France, life, comedy, or anything really. Disconnected. On the third evening it occurred to me that I needed to get out.

Next day I hired a bicycle and set off into the Camargue, that broad, even, watery plain, home to horses, bulls, mosquitoes and many breeds of bird, most famously the flamingo. I saw none of these but the flat terrain and huge skies suited my mood and my mind emptied along the straight paths beneath my spinning feet. After a couple of hours, I spotted a spire on the horizon and turned towards it. The crooked old church was now a crooked old bar, dark and gloomy after the brightness outside.

Inside, a haggard-looking old lady in black with a sad, distracted air served me a cold beer and a *sandwich jambon*. Poor old girl, she seemed even glummer than me. I decided to try out my French.

'*Est-ce que les flamandes viennent au bar?*' I enquired.

('Do you ever get flamingos coming into this bar?')

She stared at me, totally baffled.

It was not much of a gag (though I was planning to follow it up with a question about them falling over) but it seemed to poleaxe the woman. Flamingos in the bar? What was this peculiar foreigner talking about?

Then I saw it dawn on her – it was a joke! She broke into a broad if toothless smile. The thought now tickled her. Flamingos coming into her bar for a drink. Ridiculous! She started chuckling and I could see that this silly remark by a passing tourist had suddenly, somehow, reawakened in her the memory of laughter; that I had, by chance, unlocked something in her. The chuckling gave way to cackling and full-blooded hooting and her bleak introspection seemed to dissolve to reveal a wrinkled but open and beautiful old face.

After my lunch she came outside to wave me off as I set off again on my bicycle into those broad Mediterranean skies. Arriving back in Arles later I sat straight down and started writing.

It is many years now since my day in the Camargue and I am preparing for another tour of a comedy show and I will, wherever possible, stay over after the gig in a nice hotel, breakfast on porridge and kippers the next morning, then spend the day rambling in the surrounding countryside. And, at some leafy point along the way, I will no doubt remember once again the encounter with the woman in black, which has become mythic in my mind; that marvellous rejuvenated old lady, laughing, laughing, laughing.